Lessons
Unlearned

25 Years in
Customer Service

John Ragsdale

Jeff —
The customer's
not
always right!

John Ragsdale

This book is dedicated to all frontline call center agents and technical support representatives around the globe.

Table of Contents

Preface

THE CUSTOMER SERVICE INDUSTRY PLAYS A HUGE ROLE IN OUR LIVES.
Customer service influences—and sometimes dictates—every decision we make as consumers. Where we eat. What we drive. The
clothes we wear. Where we go on vacation and where we stay while
we're there. And most certainly, customer service is a major driver
of the selection of the technology we use at home and at work.

Here's a basic marketing principle: When you can't compete
on product or price, you have to compete on service. The same
quality of hotel room, the same class and feature set for an auto-
mobile, the same standard of food, all are available at similar prices
from a variety of hotel chains, auto dealers, and restaurants. So
how do you decide?

You decide based on customer service:

- You pick the hotel that you stayed at once before because
  everyone knew your name, they had complementary turn-
  down service, and when you asked if it was possible to get
  The New York Times with breakfast from room service, they
  just said "yes," not "you'll have to call the bellman for that,"
  or laugh at you (they always laugh when I ask that at Las
  Vegas hotels).

- You pick the car because they offered a free extended warranty, free service visits for the first year, a free rental car during service visits, and they'll even come pick up the car and drop it off again if you are too busy to bring it in.

- And you pick the restaurant because the servers are so friendly, the host always remembers you, and the last time you were there they brought you a free appetizer.

Customer service is of particular importance to the technology industry; customers rely on technical support services when they have a problem with a piece of hardware, software, or a consumer device. The current darling of the technology industry is Apple, and you don't have to go farther than the Genius Bar at your local Apple Store to see how Apple approaches customer service, creating a fantastic customer experience that ensures rabid fans.

Most people think of customer service as a department, and it's true—virtually every company has some sort of customer service division. But customer service is also a technology industry all on its own, with a wide array of software and hardware required to support customers with product and service questions. Enterprise technology required for large-scale customer service operations includes:

- **Customer relationship management.** Customer relationship management (CRM) is a suite of applications that creates a "360-degree view of the customer," tracking every touch point with the customer, from being a lead, through the marketing and sales cycle, to becoming a fully fledged customer entitled to customer support.

- **Knowledge management (KM).** Knowledgebases (KB) of problem/solution scenarios are common in customer support centers, providing agents with a searchable list of customer problems and how to solve them. Knowledgebases are also at the root of customer self-service websites, allowing customers to search for and resolve their own problems without calling for support.

- **Multichannel solutions.** A great deal of infrastructure is required to support customers via phone, e-mail, web chat, and online, including complex phone systems, voice menus, queuing and routing for incoming customer requests, and management dashboards to oversee operations and easily flag performance issues.

- **Customer satisfaction.** Customer satisfaction (CSAT) is definitely a huge industry on its own, ranging from online survey tools, to consulting companies specializing in satisfaction, and even complex online platforms for analyzing customer data to determine loyalty and propensity for repurchase.

- **Field service solutions.** Another subset of the customer service technology industry is field service solutions, which schedule home or office visits when repairs are needed, including intelligent routing via GPS and mobile solutions to record work performed in real time.

- **Social media.** One of the biggest changes to customer support in the last decade has been the proliferation of social media tools for customers, the most successful being online customer communities that allow customers to help other customers with product and service issues.

This book gives an insider's view of the customer service industry, providing insight for those of you battling mediocre service every day. If you understand the tools, vocabulary, and metrics that power customer service, you can definitely demand better service from your providers and understand how to appropriately deal with service issues. And for those already working in the customer service industry, hopefully this book will provide you with some new best practices, worst practices to avoid, and maybe even a laugh or two along the way.

Introduction

Twenty-five years in the customer service industry. That's quite a long stretch for an industry most people see as a stepping-stone to a "real" career in development, product management, sales, or marketing—and I've done all those roles as well, but I am always drawn back to some aspect of customer service.

Wikipedia defines customer service as "the provision of service to customers before, during and after a purchase."[1] When you ask most people what they think about customer service, they usually have a story for you, and it usually isn't positive. My nightmare customer service story (see page 5) involves a big-box building supply retailer, but I've heard incredibly bad stories involving grocery stores, clothing stores, utility companies, rental car firms, airlines, phone companies—the list goes on and on. Bad customer service is a rite of passage—a shared experience that transcends age, nationality, and education level.

While this book does not guarantee to end poor customer service, it does provide a lot of background about how to deliver customer service correctly. At the end of the day, it isn't that difficult: You ask customers what they want, and then you give it to them. But from the billions of dollars spent on processes, consultants, marketing campaigns, and technology to improve customer service levels—much of it in vain—clearly many companies struggle to effectively "ask and deliver."

I have a fairly unique view of the customer support industry because my 25 years have been divided between three different facets of the space:

- **As a practitioner.** What started as a summer job during college, working at the credit desk at JCPenney in Columbia, Missouri, turned into a 10-year career, first as a technical support representative, later becoming a team lead, then a manager for various support groups within the company, including store point of sale (POS) equipment, back-office inventory and finance applications, the corporate PC help desk, as well as supporting gas stations and grocery stores that leased credit card authorizations via the JCPenney network. My years as a practitioner allow me to help companies with operational issues, including metrics management, talent management, and process management.

- **As a vendor.** After successfully implementing a knowledgebase with dramatic return on investment (ROI) at JCPenney, I was recruited to Silicon Valley in 1995 to work for a technology start-up building knowledgebase tools for call centers. During the boom years in Silicon Valley, I worked as a systems engineer, user interface (UI) designer, product manager, and product marketing manager for customer service and CRM vendors. My years working for customer service vendors allow me to help companies understand the technology infrastructure of enterprise applications, as well as to perform use case analysis to understand the "best fit" product for a particular environment and set of business problems.

- **As an analyst.** In 2001, I joined the industry analyst ranks, first at Gideon Gartner's Giga Information Group, which was acquired by Forrester Research, and later the Service & Support Professionals Association (SSPA), now known as the

Technology Services Industry Association (TSIA). For more than a decade, I've been giving IT and business leaders advice on selecting, implementing, and using CRM, knowledge-base, and multichannel tools, as well as delivering hundreds of research reports, webcasts, and conference keynotes on customer service trends and best practices. My years working as an analyst allow me to help companies see the big picture, separate core from context, identify emerging trends and how they will impact the industry, and evaluate multiple technology tools and platforms to identify strengths and weaknesses.

This book is sort of a memoir, following along my career path as I reveal lessons learned—and unlearned—along the way, as well as personal insights and my favorite anecdotes and stories from what has so far been an amazing journey—and a journey I hope will continue for another 25 years!

Section 1

The Practitioner Years

I REMEMBER THE DAY IN 1985 WHEN THIS HUGE BOX ARRIVED IN MY office at JCPenney in Wilmington, North Carolina. I was working as the store's data entry specialist (DES), keying in data for 8 hours a day to update store merchandise inventory and pricing records, as well as pulling and distributing reports from the corporate mainframe for the store merchandise and operational managers and the accounting department, and opening the POS system each morning. In the box was an NCR PC—the first PC I'd ever used. There was no user interface; each of the programs was executed from a DOS prompt.

A few weeks later, I went to a regional training class in Fayetteville, North Carolina, with the DESs from all the JCPenney stores in our region, and learned how to use the PC. At this point, I would continue doing the bulk of my work on the data entry telex terminal, which looked like an overgrown typewriter. But JCPenney was introducing lead management for the first time, and the store departments that worked on commission (shoes, men's suits, jewelry, draperies) began collecting customer and prospect names. It was my job to enter all those names and addresses into the brand-new PC, which had a program for basic lead management, mainly creating mailing labels for the sales reps to send out personal postcards advertising upcoming sales events.

Soon after, the data entry terminal's days were numbered as JCPenney replaced the entire inventory and accounting applications I did on my teletype machine with mainframe applications accessible via a CRT screen. More regional training, more new programs to learn, and I was thrilled to be using these new tools and applications, which definitely improved speed and accuracy. As an example, updating inventory records using the telex machine was a multiday process, with my edits applied to the corporate mainframe during overnight batch processing. With the CRT applications, I was making direct edits to the mainframe data.

At that time, I was the only male DES in North Carolina, and at the tender age of 22, I was also the only DES under the age of 50. The new technology and procedures were very difficult for some of the more senior workers, some of whom had been doing the same job the same way for 20 years or more. Over the next few weeks and months, I began receiving phone calls from other stores in the region, asking me for help with the CRT applications and the PC. Working with DOS proved especially challenging for many of my peers.

JCPenney had two main corporate groups for store employees to turn to for technical assistance. The National Field Support Center (NFSC) was a technical support group based in Atlanta, responsible for supporting store POS equipment. In addition, there was the data center, another support group responsible for pulling in the POS data overnight from all of the retail stores and sending back requested inventory and accounting reports from the mainframe. When the NFSC started to build out support for PC and CRT applications, I was invited to come to Atlanta to interview for a position.

I was nervous as the interview day drew near. I was scheduled to take a 6 a.m. flight from Wilmington to Atlanta, catch a taxi to the JCPenney regional office on Peachtree Street in downtown Atlanta, spend the day interviewing, and then take a cab back to the airport and fly home at the end of the day.

I had never flown before. Other than a childhood family vacation to St. Louis, I'd never been to a big city, and certainly never on my own. I'd never even been inside a taxicab. And I was more than a little nervous about interviewing for a corporate position with these big-time corporate executives, being young and fairly naive from a tiny town in the Missouri Ozarks, now living in another small town in North Carolina.

Most of that day is a blur to me now. I remember the airplane taking off when it was still dark outside, and I was upset that I couldn't see the ocean from the air. I remember a long cab ride from the Atlanta airport to the office in bumper-to-bumper rush-hour traffic, which I thought was very cool (can you imagine?). I remember a few of the people I interviewed with that day, and how I felt I belonged there. Everyone was bright, inquisitive, had a good sense of humor, and frankly, was much younger than the average JCPenney store employee. Before I left for the airport to fly back to Wilmington, they offered me a position as a National Field Support Center technical representative. I had just a few weeks to train a replacement, pack up everything, and move to Atlanta. Life would never be the same again.

I've seen a lot of changes in technology support since 1985. The team of operators used to screen incoming calls has been replaced by an intelligent voice response (IVR) system. Incredibly slow and painful-to-use mainframe trouble-ticketing systems have been replaced with CRM web applications offering subsecond response time. My four shelves of manuals with hundreds of yellow sticky notes have been replaced with a searchable knowledgebase. Pure phone operations have evolved to include e-mail, chat, web self-service, and now, social networking.

Interestingly, though, many things have remained the same. The same metrics that measured personal, team, and department performance are still used today. Soft skills (or customer service skills) training is virtually the same as 1980s training—only there is usually less of it today. Keeping up the morale of employees who spend all day hearing other people's problems is as big a challenge today as it was then.

Or maybe it is even a bigger challenge today. Customer attention spans grow shorter; patience is in short supply. Customers used to call a support desk with a sort of reverence, knowing they were speaking to the experts. Today, people are more tech savvy, more time-sensitive, and let's face it, more demanding and aggressive. The Internet has created oceans of supposed "experts," in some way devaluing the reputation of technical support representatives.

A couple of years ago, I did a consumer survey with Lithium Technologies, a community platform vendor, to find out how demographics impact customer service channel preferences (channels are the routes customers take to access support—by phone, e-mail, chat, or online). The results were what you would expect: The younger the customer, the less likely they were to use a phone, and the more likely they were to use a social networking avenue or web chat to solve a problem. But there was one finding from that survey, as seen in *Figure 1.1*, that really surprised me, and I think it illustrates the challenges ahead for customer support.

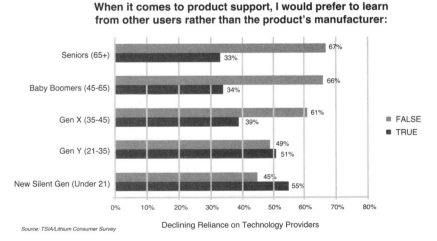

Figure 1.1: Declining Reliance on Technology Providers

Seniors, those aged 65 or older, are very reliant on technology providers for support, with 67 percent saying they prefer support from the product manufacturer. But look at what happens with younger customers. The New Silent Generation, or NSG, those under 21, definitely lean the other way, with the majority, 55 percent, saying that they prefer to seek product help from other users. I would even go so far as to say that younger customers are *distrustful* of product providers. In a social media world, technology support teams have become "The Man," the big establishment, concerned about profit, not people.

And maybe they are right. I hate waiting in long hold queues listening to advertisements playing over and over, and support agents sometimes spend more time upselling me on products and services than they do helping me with my problem. Poor service and overly aggressive sales tactics can definitely take the reverence out of calling technical support.

I talk to many companies about customer service, and I frequently give speeches at technology conferences about the state of the industry and trends in service. Everyone always asks me if I have a nightmare customer service story, so before the next chapter kicks off with advice to improve service, I thought I would take a moment to talk about bad service. Really bad service. Here's my story.

The Home Depot Debacle

I was gutting and remodeling my master bath and the guest bath, with a project budget around $50,000. (Wow, moving plumbing is really expensive!) I found a vanity, countertop, sink, and fixtures I liked at the local Home Depot. I let them know I was starting a big project, and they agreed to hold the items and deliver them. I paid for the merchandise, as well as the delivery fee, and scheduled the delivery about 2 weeks out.

At the time, Home Depot was opening up a chain of higher-end building supply and furnishing stores called the EXPO Design Center. In fact, the first Bay Area EXPO store was soon opening about 45 minutes away from me in Palo Alto, California. About a week after I purchased the bathroom vanity and related products, I received a call from Home Depot, and here's what they said: "The items you purchased are now going to be carried exclusively through our EXPO stores. You need to come into Home Depot, get a refund for the purchase, then drive up to Palo Alto and repurchase the merchandise."

I was already about to explode, but they hadn't even gotten to the good part yet. "The price for the items will be higher at EXPO, so just to let you know, you will have to pay an additional few hundred dollars. Oh, and the delivery fee from Palo Alto will be three times as much." And they hung up. I called back, talked to just about everyone in the store, and couldn't get anyone to listen to me. I thought surely if they just listened to themselves they would realize how ridiculous they were being. But, no.

In my opinion, the worst thing a company can do to a customer is to not listen. I am the first one to admit that the customer is *not* always right. But if you don't take the time to listen to what they are saying and at least try to understand their frustration, you will never solve the problem.

I was forced to go into the store, and still received the same disinterested runaround. There comes a point in these situations when customers say to themselves, "I have two choices. I can shut up, do what they want, and get taken advantage of. Or I can make a scene." In this instance, I didn't want to make a scene. I hate making a scene. But I really was left with no alternative.

So, when I finally got face-to-face with the store manager, I recapped the situation and let the manager know that I had my receipt showing I legally owned the merchandise and they needed to deliver it as agreed or my contractor could pick up the merchandise immediately. By the time I finished, other customers overheard the exchange and a small crowd had formed. The other shoppers loudly encouraged me, telling me to seek legal advice and to not accept "no" as an answer.

Finally, the store manager begrudgingly said the merchandise would be delivered as scheduled, and it turned out it had never left their store anyway—it was still sitting in the customer "to be delivered" area. I guess they were just seeing if I was gullible enough to be conned into paying more for the same merchandise.

Just to recap how costly this situation was for the retailer, Home Depot knew I was at the beginning of a large remodeling project, and I made sure they didn't see another cent from that project. My contractor went to smaller local suppliers, and I didn't mind paying an extra 10 percent for some materials, just to be sure Home Depot received nothing more from me.

What lessons can we draw from this nightmare customer service story? Here are a few recommendations for any retail or product company working directly with customers that would have eliminated or at least diffused my situation:

- **Empower employees to question policy.** A company policy on returns, repairs, or any service issue may have been crafted with the utmost care, but there are sometimes extenuating circumstances that make the policy unfair for customers. Customer-facing employees must be trained to evaluate each scenario individually and ask themselves, "Is this fair for the customer? If I were the customer, would I think it was fair?" If the answer is no, the service representative should be empowered to remedy the situation as quickly and easily as possible. In my example, the fact that the store had decided to transfer certain merchandise to a different brand and charge more was certainly within their right, but the decision should never have been applied to past purchases. Someone should have put that through their "fairness litmus test," and I should never have been contacted in the first place.

- **Avoid public showdowns with customers.** When dealing with customers in public—whether in a retail or grocery store, the post office, or a restaurant—if a customer is prepared to fight over an issue, you should move the conversation off the floor and into a quieter area or even a manager's office. If the customer is unreasonable, there is no point ruining the customer experience for everyone else. If the customer has a valid point, other customers will often speak up and further inflame the situation. At the very least, every customer who overhears the exchange will tell all their friends what happened, negatively impacting the brand.

- **Consider the lifetime value of the customer in every decision.** When it comes to customers, companies have to take a long-term view. How much will this customer spend with us over their lifetime? If there is potential for considerable business in the future, the company should be wary of alienating the customer or giving them any reason to take that future business elsewhere. This includes siding with the customer on minor issues to make the problem go away, illustrating to the customer that you value their business and want to keep them coming back.

There is one final coda to this story. In January 2009, Home Depot announced that they were shutting their EXPO business, laying off 7,000 employees.[1] Today, all that "high-end" merchandise is right back on Home Depot shelves, where it always belonged.

1 | Stewardship

stew·ard·ship (noun)
ˈstü-ərd-ˌship, ˈstyü-; ˈst(y)ürd
    1. *the office, duties, and obligations of a steward*
    2. *the conducting, supervising, or managing of something; especially:*
       the careful and responsible management of something entrusted to
       one's care <stewardship of natural resources>[1]

I'VE BEEN LUCKY TO HAVE SOME AMAZING MANAGERS IN MY CAREER. When JCPenney decided to build a new corporate headquarters in Dallas, they relocated many corporate operations, including the old headquarters on Sixth Avenue in New York, as well as the IT and development teams, which had always been located in the Atlanta regional office. NFSC was part of that relocation, and while many of my Atlanta coworkers opted not to make the move, I accepted a transfer and a promotion, reporting to work in Dallas as a team manager. The founder of the NFSC, Herm Brinkman, was near retirement and did not make the move to Dallas. Our new manager was a former JCPenney store manager from the Seattle area, Dean Wortham.

I will never again have a manager as kind and caring as Dean Wortham. As a newly minted manager, I needed help, and in his always-patient way, Dean taught me a lot about being a good manager, and a few lessons about being a good person as well.

As Dean assumed management of the NFSC, renaming the Dallas incarnation the Store Systems Hotline, or SSH, he talked to the management team—and the entire department—about stewardship. Stewardship meant that there was no more "us and them" attitude about customers. We were responsible for these stores and their customers. If the point of sale systems went down, it cost stores—and the company—thousands of dollars a minute in lost revenue. Dean helped us all reconnect to the stores, not as overlords, or even slightly superior corporate employees, but as caretakers, parents, big brothers and sisters. We grew to have a new attitude toward store employees as we felt personally invested in their success—a much different scenario than being a condescending support representative.

Love the Customer

Dean started two campaigns to build an environment of stewardship. The first was "Love the Customer." In the Atlanta days of NFSC, most of the support techs had some background with JCPenney stores, either having moved up through the store ranks as I had, or having worked with stores in another JCPenney corporate department, such as the catalog or controllers division, before coming to NFSC. We had been through the customer service training provided to store employees, we had an intimate relationship with the retail side of the business—and firsthand knowledge of retail customers—so the concept of stewardship, and loving the customer, came pretty easy.

Unfortunately, instilling the concept of stewardship into some of the new employees at the Dallas Store Systems Hotline was more difficult. Since the majority of NFSC employees did not make the move to Dallas, we had to hire a large team of support technicians very fast. And instead of the traditional approach of recruiting tech-savvy store and corporate employees, we hired newly minted graduates with degrees from a technical school that operates as a degree mill. Having no history with the company, no familiarity with the company's retail operations, and no "working their way up" to land a tech support job, these employees did not empathize with store employees; in fact, they tended to be condescending. They didn't love the customer; they treated them as an interruption. And many of these new hires were very open about not planning to work in tech support for more than 1 to 2 years before expecting a promotion to a development role. Their current job was beneath them.

For those of us who saw working at the support center as a desirable job, dealing with these "short timers" wasn't easy. They didn't value the work we did, and as a result, they didn't have a very good work ethic about being on time, customer service skills, or employee productivity. While Dean's Love the Customer campaign was more challenging than I initially thought, we did turn some of those employees around. How? We had store employees come in for tours and talk about what happened at the store level when the registers went down. We took groups of support techs on tours of local JCPenney stores so support employees could better understand the retail operation and the stress of having face-to-face customers. We had district and regional managers come in to talk to the support techs about the importance of technology and the role of the Store Systems Hotline.

If you want employees to love the customer, you have to start with employees who are capable of loving someone—besides themselves. This meant we needed to hire the right support techs in the first place, and after that initial crowd of new college grads, we started incorporating more screening for customer service, soft skills, temperament, and attitude into the hiring process. And we expanded training to include more guidance on working with customers, including phone training using real scenarios of difficult problems and difficult customers.

This was not the last time I encountered support employees who did not have the people skills for the job. In fact, in later years when implementing knowledgebases for support centers around the globe and doing audits of support center best practices as an analyst, I've frequently found support groups with multiple employees having bad attitudes about a support role and some level of condescension for the customers. In these environments, there is a whole of set of problems I know I will find, including CSAT challenges and high employee turnover.

The Technology Services Industry Association (TSIA) asks members a survey question about which support employee skills have the most impact on performance reviews, and the results are interesting, as seen in *Figure 1.1.1.*

Technical knowledge is the single most important employee skill, rated higher than customer service skills, customer satisfaction surveys, quality monitoring data, and productivity. Personally, I think this is the root of many problems in our industry— overreliance on technical ability and shortchanging customer service or "soft" skills. My time at JCPenney showed me that non-technical employees with fantastic people skills and an aptitude toward technology can easily be taught complex technology. But technology whizzes with little or no social skills will never become warm and empathetic on the phone, no matter how much soft-skills training they receive.

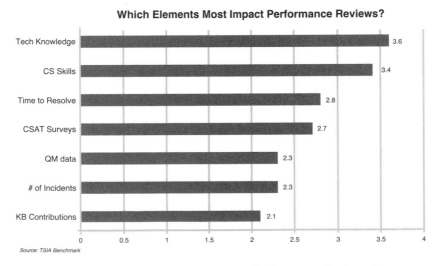

Figure 1.1.1: Which Elements Most Impact Performance Reviews?

Love the Employee

Dean's second campaign to build the concept of stewardship was for us managers: "Love the Employee." A departure from the traditional autocratic view of the manager/employee relationship, Dean wanted us to recognize employees as people and make sure they were fulfilled in work and in life—within our power of influence, of course. We started multiple programs designed to recognize and celebrate employees, including an Employee of the Month program, complete with an annual dinner to name Employee of the Year.

At the time, I was attending night school, working on my degree in management, learning about the then-popular Theories X, Y, and Z, and I was eager to try out new programs to recognize and reward employees. One of the popular theories at the time was "management by walking around," which meant getting out of your office to interact more with employees, understand their workload and performance better, and hopefully coach them on small issues before they turned into big issues.

Dean encouraged management by walking around, as well as another popular management approach at the time, "catch them doing something right." We had certificates for a free lunch or a free muffin from the company cafeteria printed up, and when an employee went above and beyond, we immediately rewarded them with a certificate. Some employees were so happy to be acknowledged that they stapled those certificates to their cubicle walls instead of cashing them in.

Not only did these programs help improve morale, but they also gave us managers a much better idea of what was really going on among our teams. Dean Wortham had fostered an environment in which employees felt comfortable asking for help, and the reward systems turned out to provide positive reinforcement for the desired behavior, so some of the undesired behavior lessened over time. I certainly felt more personally invested in the needs of my employees because of Dean's Love the Employee campaign, and I think I've become a much better manager over the years because I learned early on to treat employees like people first, and to think of them as individuals—not cogs in the wheel.

Another valuable lesson I learned from Dean is that giving employees correct assessments of their performance on evaluations was incredibly important. Part of loving the employee is giving them factual, actionable, and constructive feedback, and sometimes a little tough love is required.

I had inherited an employee who was a bit of bully, and while she was a knowledgeable support technician, she was rough around the edges, difficult to work with, and flew into a rage when offered any constructive feedback. As a result, for years she had been given higher marks than she deserved on performance reviews because managers were afraid of the tirade that would erupt if they rated her below "exceeds." I was not afraid of the tirade and gave her a fair assessment of her performance. There were tears, there was shouting, and there was an uncomfortable tension for about a month afterward. But ultimately, the feedback helped.

We had a lot of problems with employee performance evaluation "inflation" at that time, including some of the degree-mill "short timers" whose managers rated them higher than they deserved so as to not create conflicts in the workplace. In other words, these employees did not take constructive criticism well since they thought the job was beneath them anyway, so managers gave them higher ratings than they deserved in order to avoid arguments.

It turns out that many managers approach performance reviews hoping to avoid drama—that inevitable blowup that occurs when an employee is faced with an assessment that in no way matches their own self-assessment. If you love your employees, you are truthful with them. If you don't point out their growth areas, they won't grow, and they become bitter over time as they feel more isolated and unappreciated, yet have no constructive feedback on how to improve. However, employees should never be blindsided by a performance review. Whether it is uncomfortable or not, managers must give ongoing coaching to employees, including constructive criticism. Employees should never be confronted with a performance issue for the first time during the annual review.

I think about customer service and stewardship a great deal today, especially when as a customer I receive treatment that clearly indicates I'm not dealing with someone who has ever been told to "love the customer." The bored or impatient phone rep who sighs when you ask a question. The retail employee who ignores you at the register because she is talking or texting on her iPhone. The restaurant server who rolls his eyes when you ask for something. Honestly, as a customer, I don't feel the love all that often.

After all these years, when I look back at Dean Wortham's leadership, I realize how lucky I was to have learned some key lessons so early on in my management career, and I hope I can pass some of them along to you. So consider this your first lesson: If you don't have the capacity within yourself to love the customer *and* your employees, then customer service is definitely not the career for you.

« Key Lessons Learned from Chapter 1 »

It takes a special person to be a customer service star. You have to be empathetic. You have to be patient. And you have to be able to love the customer, every day, on every interaction. Indoctrinating support employees from Day One that their primary job is stewardship is a great way to promote the right attitude. With that in mind, I would like to recap some key lessons learned from this chapter:

- **Support as stewardship.** Support employees often become lost in all the performance metrics related to the job and forget about the human side of customer interactions. The role of a support employee is to be a steward for customers—a caretaker, a trusted advisor, a lifeline when things go wrong. This is a serious obligation, and you should screen prospective employees to see if they are able to accept this obligation willingly.

- **Not everyone is empathetic.** If you want employees to love the customer, you have to start with employees who are capable of loving someone—besides themselves. When interviewing prospective support agents or technicians, look for volunteer work, social interests, awareness of world or political events, or tight ties to family and friends. All of these indicate the candidate is not self-absorbed and has the potential to be a steward to your customers.

- **Importance of ongoing soft-skills training.** Many technology firms overemphasize technical ability and shortchange customer service or "soft" skills. While answering a question correctly is critically important, if the employee can't communicate effectively with the customer, the interaction will be uncomfortable for everyone involved. Soft-skills training is important up front, with refreshers annually, as well as ongoing coaching for employees whose satisfaction scores indicate that they are not connecting with customers or are not being perceived as caring.

- **Recognize and celebrate employees.** Managers often forget what it was like fielding calls and e-mails from upset customers for 8 hours a day. Support employees have a stressful and emotionally draining job, and they need to know that they are appreciated and valued. Since they don't always receive that positive reinforcement from customers, it is your job as a manager to provide it.

- **Catch them doing something right.** Managers are trained to look for infractions of rules, policies, or recognized best practices and immediately correct the behavior. But don't get so caught up in policing for bad behavior that you forget to celebrate great behavior. What I have learned is that instead of correcting people doing something wrong, it is sometimes more effective to identify a worker doing something correctly and hold them up as an example. You get the same point across without singling out anyone for being incorrect.

- **Offer factual, actionable, and constructive feedback.** No one should ever find out that they are doing something wrong by reading a performance review. Whether you have formal one-on-one time scheduled with employees or you handle feedback on an ad hoc basis, address small issues before they become bigger issues and don't pull punches with constructive feedback. But remember that feedback must be constructive. Don't just say what they did wrong—instead, explain why it is a problem and how to do it correctly. If employees understand the positive business impact of the correct behavior, it is easier for them to comply.

TALES FROM THE VAULT: MAGIC SLATE THERAPY

Let's face it: There are a lot of rude people out there, and unfortunately, sometimes they need support. Regardless of how much training or experience you have in dealing with difficult customers, sometimes they can really get under your skin. It is important that employees have some way to release frustrations when handling rude, condescending, aggressive, hostile, and sometimes profane customers.

An easy and low-cost solution is what I call Magic Slate Therapy, which I learned from LuAnn Rollins, a coworker from the JCPenney NFSC in Atlanta. Remember those magic slates from your childhood? Some kind of clipboard affair with a sheet of plastic you could write on and your words appear, and then by pulling up the sheet of plastic, everything is completely erased?

LuAnn and I both kept magic slates in our desks, and when we were on the phone with a real piece of work, we would write exactly what kind of person they were in big letters on that slate and hold it up high so everyone could see. We instantly received thumbs-ups and "hang in theres" from teammates, and by venting, we were able to release the anger and concentrate on solving the problem and hopefully getting the customer back on track as quickly as possible.

Over the years I've bought dozens of magic slates for my support employees, sometimes to use in coaching sessions on dealing with difficult customers. I still think it is a simple and lighthearted approach to workplace stress, and unlike e-mail and chat, with a magic slate, there's no audit trail.

2 | Metrics

As a new technical support manager, one of my assigned duties was printing phone reports. Back in 1990, this meant going to a teletype terminal for our then-state-of-the-art ROLM 9000 phone system and printing all the reports from the previous day, which detailed productivity statistics for each employee—the number of calls received and placed, average call length, amount of time "off phone" researching a problem—as well as overall call statistics such as volume by time, time spent holding in queue, calls by team, etc. I also printed weekly and monthly reports.

I took this big stack of reports and dutifully put them in big blue binders and placed them on a bookshelf, never to be seen or used again. We must have used those reports, or at least I'd like to think we used them, but I have to admit I have no recollection of ever looking at those reports or using the data in any way. This is a standard way that new support managers are introduced to the world of metrics: You are shown where all the reports are filed, probably your own version of big binders on a shelf somewhere, and are left to figure it all out on your own.

I have a love-hate relationship with metrics. As an analyst, I love metrics, because the data can be used to not only identify top and bottom performers, but also to track changes in metrics in order to calculate ROI for new technology projects or new processes, as well as to identify trends in both problems and customer behavior.

But I also hate metrics, because some managers become so immersed in specific numbers that they lose sight of the overall operation. The sheer number of metrics is so high—TSIA tracks over 300 metrics in the support services benchmark survey—that it isn't hard to lose sight of the forest because of all the trees. And employees receive such conflicting messages on metrics, with companies launching a program to improve one metric this month, another metric next month, with no real understanding of what influences each metric and what the actual benefit of moving a metric up or down may be.

I also think customers deserve a basic understanding of support metrics, because if they understand how support techs are incented and graded, it will help them understand—and hopefully manipulate—support processes, escalations, and overall handling of their incident.

With all the existing metrics and new metrics emerging with social media, I can't possibly cover every known metric and how to use them in this chapter, so instead, I will focus on a high-level look at metrics and how they interrelate, and common metrics used by most support organizations.

Here is the core thing about customer service metrics that I wish I had known early in my management career: Metrics are divided into three categories, and keeping all three categories in balance should be the goal of every support manager. The three categories are quality metrics, financial metrics, and operational metrics.

Quality Metrics: Monitoring Customer Satisfaction and Loyalty

Quality metrics are metrics that measure the level of support quality delivered to customers. Most companies tend to focus a great deal of attention on customer satisfaction and loyalty as the most important quality metrics, although other metrics also contribute to the quality of service delivery, including adherence to service level agreements (SLAs), quality monitoring data from third-party workforce management solutions, number of product defects, and programs such as NetPromoter™. At a minimum, I recommend that companies track the following quality metrics:

- **Post-incident surveys by channel.** When an incident closes, customers should be surveyed about their experience. Surveys should be executed for all supported customer channels (phone, e-mail, chat, web self-service) to be certain that quality is consistent across touch points. For assisted support surveys, customers should be surveyed about multiple aspects of the interaction, including customer service skills, technical knowledge, completeness of solution provided, time to respond and resolve, and satisfaction with the incident overall. To receive the highest response rate from satisfaction surveys, it is critical to send the survey as soon as possible after the interaction, such as prompting the customer with a survey at the end of a remote-control session, or using a rule to e-mail a survey when an incident is set to a closed status. It is also important that enough metadata is collected about each interaction to allow satisfaction scores to be filtered by product, geography, employee type, etc.

- **Self-service and/or community experience.** It is also important to survey customers about their self-service experiences. I recommend prompting customers with a short survey as they exit your self-service site or online community, or sending a short survey via e-mail after a session, asking if they found the answer they needed and if they have any suggestions to make the site more useful. These surveys can be used to calculate the rate of self-service success as well as document how many issues are being deflected to unassisted channels.

- **Periodic relationship surveys.** These quarterly or annual surveys measure your overall relationship with the customer, not specific support interactions. Additionally, in enterprise accounts, relationship surveys go to the account holder, such as the vice president of service or even a CIO, while transactional surveys go to system administrators, providing a balanced view from all levels of the account. Individual questions on the survey should ask about overall support experience, satisfaction with products, and value received from products and services.

- **Customer loyalty.** Customer satisfaction is important to track, but no formula exists to show exactly how a rise in satisfaction impacts the bottom line. To help link the customer experience to revenue, it is important to ask customers the loyalty question: *Do you intend to continue purchasing products from this vendor?* This one question may tell you more about the health of your accounts and their future profitability than any other metric. Any customer who says no to this question should be immediately referred to an account manager so that he can be made aware of any issues thwarting customer success. Interestingly, according to the TSIA benchmark, the results of the loyalty question and the promoter question (*Will you recommend us to your peers?*) are quite different, as seen in *Figure 1.2.1*.

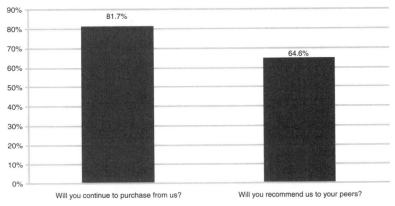

Source: TSIA Benchmark

Figure 1.2.1: Loyal Customers Not Necessarily Promoters

While these are the basic quality metrics, some companies are becoming very creative with customer satisfaction tracking, and I have to admit, sometimes that creativity worries me. In recent years, more companies are building "customer success indexes," which pull data from multiple sources to create an index rating for each customer. While I admire the complexity of the model, some of these indexes seem so convoluted that moving a few points up or down doesn't give you a reason for the change without breaking down the formulas to see what is happening behind the scenes.

My advice: Be as creative as you want with developing a satisfaction or success index, but continue tracking the core metrics, as well, for benchmarking purposes. You can never identify how you compare to your industry peers if everyone is using a customized index.

Financial Metrics: Monitoring Profitability

Financial metrics are those that track operational costs, including revenue generated through service delivery and gross margins for service operations. Though in the early days of support many companies considered customer service a cost center, today's technical support and consumer call centers calculate gross margins based on maintenance and additional services revenue minus costs. I recommend that companies track the following cost metrics:

- **Gross margin.** The gross margin represents the percent of total services revenue that the service organization retains after incurring the direct costs associated with service operations. The higher the percentage, the more the company retains of each dollar of revenue. With value-added services creating additional services revenue from premier support options and upsell/cross-sell, service and support margins are becoming a very visible metric—even to Wall Street.

- **Hourly labor burden rate.** I recommend calculating labor burden rate as follows: salary or wages + overtime + cost of employee benefits including facility and equipment costs + cost of applicable taxes. In the U.S., use 2,080 hours per year as the standard number of available work hours per year to derive your hourly rate for this metric. Calculate the average for each level or tier. Not only can the average hourly rate be benchmarked, but it also can be used to calculate other metrics, such as cost per incident or cost per issue.

- **Fully burdened cost per incident.** Average cost per incident divides total costs by number of incidents resolved during that period. Average cost should be calculated for each supported channel using infrastructure costs for the channel and average time worked per channel. More mature organizations have more granular cost metrics, such as by incident type or failing component, useful when calculating cost savings for deflecting specific issues to self-service.

- **Training days per year.** With agent customer service and technical skills contributing to overall productivity and customer satisfaction, measuring the amount of training provided to support employees is helpful to ensure adequate training without over-reaching on cost.

Operational Metrics: Monitoring Speed of Delivery

Operational metrics are those typically associated with speed or velocity of delivery and are usually captured by telephony systems for phone calls, multichannel management platforms for e-channels, incident management systems, or remote support platforms. In order to understand interaction volumes and their impact on service delivery, companies should track the following operational metrics:

- **Incident volume by channel.** Understanding incident volume trends is critical for staffing plans and quality control to ensure you have enough support technicians available to handle inbound volume. Each company will find unique patterns in volume peaks, with Mondays and Fridays often the busiest days; companies that support accounting systems typically see peaks around tax deadlines; retail firms see peaks associated with holiday seasons. Incident volume must be tracked for every supported customer channel, including phone, e-mail, web, web chat, and social media.

- **Hold time and abandon rates.** A major contributor to customer satisfaction, hold time measures the amount of time customers spend in a phone or web chat queue waiting for an available agent. As hold times extend, customers lose patience and hang up the phone. The percent of callers who hang up before reaching a live person is the abandon rate. As hold times rise, so do abandon rates.

- **Incident handling time, average talk time.** This metric tracks the average time support technicians spend talking to customers or working on an incident. More experienced support techs can resolve issues faster, lowering talk time or handling time. Managers should monitor these metrics to identify if employees need additional training in technology or customer service skills—sometimes coaching on how to close the conversation may be helpful.

- **Response and resolution rates.** Response time measures the amount of time it takes customers to reach a support technician; resolution rates measure the average time elapsed before an incident is closed. It is important to track metrics by channel. Many companies give phone incidents priority treatment, ignoring e-mail or web incidents until phone volume drops. Also, being able to identify response and resolution times by problem type will help indicate when additional training may be needed to speed issue resolution.

Resolution time tracking is becoming more complicated, as companies try to separate resolution time for customer issues that support can resolve, compared to issues requiring action beyond support's control. For customer problems requiring a bug fix or enhancement request, some companies close the ticket as resolved to a future fix, while others track the problem as unresolved until a new release or patch is delivered.

Personally, I consider the issue resolved if a bug or enhancement request has been created for the request, but I do understand tracking the longer-term resolution time for companies making the link between issue resolution and customer satisfaction and loyalty. If you do prefer to track issue resolution time when a code change is required, at least be able to track these resolution times separately from issues closed by support.

- **First-contact resolution.** A key contributor to customer satisfaction, first-contact resolution (or FCR) means the first support tech the customer speaks with solves their problem on the first interaction—an ideal support scenario. Typically, incidents resolved on the first contact are also less expensive for the organization, as incident-handling time is shorter. FCR rates should also be tracked by channel. When e-mail or web incidents have low FCR, it may mean additional required fields should be added to collect more information from the customer up front, eliminating the need for multiple interactions to gather needed data.

- **Escalation rates.** Escalation rates are a major contributor to incident cost. Most support organizations have multiple levels or tiers of support techs, with higher levels offering greater expertise. Incidents that must be escalated to Level 2 or Level 3 cost more, not only because incidents are open longer, but because these more expert support techs have higher salaries. Support management should identify issues being escalated that could be resolved at a lower tier with additional training or knowledgebase content, ideally shifting a higher percentage of employees to the less expensive Level 1 over time.

- **Incidents resolved within 24 hours.** In the minds of customers, if an issue can't be resolved on the first contact, the next best thing is having it resolved the same day. This metric may depend on what service level agreements are in place, as many companies have a commitment in customer SLAs to attempt to resolve issues within 1 day, if possible. Also contributing to customer satisfaction, support management should track when average issue resolution stretches beyond 24 hours. As with previous metrics, track the percent of issues resolved in 24 hours by channel to ensure e-mail or web incidents aren't being ignored.

Balancing Quality, Financial, and Operational Metrics

Balancing quality, financial, and operational metrics is what most managers spend their time doing, though most don't realize it in those terms. And failure to understand the importance of this balance leads to many of the wrong-headed decisions made by support management.

When managers don't understand balancing quality, financial, and operational metrics, problems occur. An all-too-frequent example is when a company decides it has to raise customer satisfaction scores.

Referring to *Figure 1.2.2*, if you want to improve this quality metric, you have to look at the impact on financial and operational metrics. The first approach to improving CSAT is usually additional customer service, or soft skills, training. This not only adds to employee costs, but taking agents off the phone for training will impact operational metrics as well. Another approach is coaching employees to spend more time with customers, practice "active listening," and make sure they are thorough in resolving the problem. This approach extends a key velocity metric, average talk time, meaning each call takes longer, agents handle fewer calls per shift, and without increasing head count, customers hold longer in the phone queue and service levels decline.

Figure 1.2.2: Balancing Quality, Financial, and Operational Metrics

This doesn't mean companies shouldn't try to improve CSAT. But to change one metric, you have to understand the inter-dependencies with all the other metrics and acknowledge that moving one metric impacts several others—for better or worse. Figuring this out at the start of every project can help you select a project direction with the fewest negative impacts, or at least factor the expected impact on metrics into the hiring plan and department budget.

The Importance of Baseline Metrics

When I talk to companies about specific metrics, I often hear that the support organization isn't collecting that metric today because they know they need to improve. If you wait until all of your metrics are "best in class" before measuring them, you'll have a very long wait. In fact, if you don't start tracking metrics when you are in trouble, you'll never be able to measure how much you are improving.

As a technology analyst, one of the primary ways I use metrics is to calculate return on investment for technology projects. I research which technologies impact which metrics, and help companies understand what metric improvements are realistic to expect with a new technology deployment. It is surprising to me how many companies do not establish baseline metrics before launching a big technology project, so they have no way to measure the impact of the project. Without before and after metrics, you cannot calculate the ROI for any new tool, making project success a very subjective thing.

The CRM industry has been plagued for years by doomsday articles claiming things like "70 percent of CRM customers don't receive the anticipated value from the project"—sometimes spun by headline-seeking journalists as "70 percent of CRM projects fail." To this oft-quoted statistic, I have a one-word rebuttal: *bullshit*. CRM technology does not revolutionize the way you do business, but it does enforce processes that tend to streamline operations and provide management reporting so small problems can be spotted before they become big problems.

I've talked to hundreds of companies about their CRM experience, and those who say they didn't receive the anticipated value usually did not have baseline metrics in place before the project, so they were not able to measure if or how much the implementation improved productivity or efficiency. Additionally, unhappy CRM customers often blamed the software for internal process problems—but more on that topic in a later chapter.

« Key Lessons Learned from Chapter 2 »

For new support managers, the number of metrics tracked by your organization can be overwhelming. A good starting point is to ask your management peers which metrics they track closely and why, which will help you find a place to focus in the beginning. As a recap, some key lessons learned from this chapter are:

- **Customers deserve a basic understanding of support metrics.** Without going into too much detail about your operational practices, customers should know which metrics are important to you so they better understand how you operate. Highlighting key metrics and your goals can be effectively communicated in customer service level agreements. On an ongoing basis, update customers on your performance with key metrics, as well as any action plans to improve metrics that are visible to customers, such as first-contact resolution and satisfaction scores.

- **There are three categories of metrics tracked by support organizations.** Quality metrics are those that measure the level of support quality delivered to customers. Financial metrics track operational costs, including revenue generated through service delivery and gross margins for service operations. Operational metrics are those typically associated with speed or velocity of service delivery.

- **Balancing quality, financial, and operational metrics.** Keeping all three categories of support metrics in balance should be the goal of every support manager. Remember that metrics are interrelated, so moving one metric up or down will impact related metrics. Figuring this out at the start of every project can help you select a project direction with the fewest negative impacts, or at least factor the expected impact on metrics into the hiring plan and department budget.

Many times in my career I've seen support organizations go overboard to improve one metric without understanding what the impact will be in other areas. One of my favorite stories on this topic comes from a major U.S. airline whose call center management decided that its average phone call length was getting too long. The company announced to its agents what the desired call length was, and let them know that they would be marked down on their next performance review if their average call length was over this "limit," which, if I recall correctly, was in the 3-minute range. The thinking was that by cutting the length of each phone call, the same amount of agents could handle a higher volume of calls, and callers would spend less time in the hold queue waiting for an available agent.

The call center agents responded, and when they saw that a phone call was reaching the 3-minute mark, they did whatever they could to end the call: They told the customer to think about it and call back. They let them know they could browse options online and call back when ready. They would tell them anything to just get them off the phone before 3 minutes were up so they wouldn't hear about it from their manager.

So what happened? Yes, average call length dropped, so the agents were handling more calls, being more productive, and customers experienced shorter hold times. Everyone wins, right?

Wrong. By cutting conversations short as they reached an arbitrary time limit, revenue dropped as customers didn't complete reservations fast enough and were told to call back. Customer satisfaction scores plummeted as customers felt rushed off the phone—which they were. And hotel and rental car partners complained because their inbound volume dropped due to the fact that the airline agents were not completing any airline reservations and therefore weren't offering an option for the customer to be transferred to a hotel or rental car partner.

By fixating on one metric—average talk time—customer support management cut revenue for themselves and their partners, and irritated customers to boot. Before launching any initiative to move a single metric, think through what other metrics will be impacted and what the longer-term impacts to the overall organizational will be.

3 | Managing and Motivating Support Employees

As I said, I've had some great managers over the years. I've also had a few really lousy ones. Looking back, I'd say one of the key differences between a good manager and a bad manager is his or her desire and ability to motivate me. The manager who asked each week in our one-on-one meeting why I was so fat was clearly not helping my attitude toward my job. The manager who continually took credit for my ideas, without even a word of thanks, made me secretive and less trustful toward managers. The manager who passed me over (twice) for a promotion because I wasn't married with children showed me that hard work doesn't necessarily pay off.

Like most technical support managers, I got my job because I was a really good technical support agent. But the skill sets required by the two roles could not be more different, and succeeding at one role in no way makes you automatically a success at the other. Not only did I not have the first idea about how to be a manager, but I was managing the team I had worked on for years, so the team had a difficult time seeing me as their coworker one day and their manager the next (a terrible position in which to put a first-time manager). Since my strength lay in solving technical problems, I spent the first year micromanaging the team, reading every incident, and telling them how I would have handled the situation. This did not endear me to the team, to the say the least.

With time, lots of mentoring, and a great deal of formal training and education, I do think I have become a good manager. I've learned you can lead people easier than you can push them, recognizing employees as people first helps tremendously, and if you can't find a way to motivate each employee each week, you're not doing your job.

For new technical support managers, I want to pass along some of what I've learned to help you come up to speed faster. This chapter includes some lessons learned—and unlearned— about employee relations.

The first step is to recognize that people are individuals. The most frustrating thing for me as a manager is when an employee's thought processes don't work the same way mine do. People process information at different speeds and require different kinds of explanations. You can never assume an employee knows something, regardless of how simple or basic. And you have to be able to interact with each employee uniquely, depending on their personality, sense of humor, educational level, and the like.

While it is true that everyone is different, over the years I have identified several "types," which seem to represent the majority of support employees I've encountered. If you can learn to identify each type and understand how to communicate effectively with and motivate each type, your job as a manager will be much easier. The four technical support employee types are: The Slammer, The Geek, The Socialite, and The Creative. All have pros and cons, and each one has unique challenges for communication and motivation, as seen in *Figure 1.3.1.*

Four Technical Support Employee Types

Figure 1.3.1: Four Technical Support Employee Types

The Slammer

I'm starting with The Slammer because I have the most experience with this type . . . because I am one. The name "Slammer" comes from a telecommunications phrase for a tele-salesperson who accepts an offer on your behalf without your permission, which used to be a common practice with long-distance carriers who would "slam" customers into an agreement with a new carrier without their consent.

I found out I was a Slammer very early in my career when I was taking JCPenney catalog orders over the phone from customers. We were encouraged to have orders shipped directly to customers, but at that time, most customers wanted to pick up the package at the store to avoid shipping fees. In addition, they could return the item instantly if they didn't like it or it didn't fit. I found that instead of offering the customer a choice for direct shipping, it was easier just to close the call with, "Your order will be shipped directly to you in 3 to 5 days. Thank you for your order." And hang up before they could argue.

After a few customers called back to complain, my Slamming habit was nipped in the bud very quickly by my manager, who admired my ingenuity in upping our direct-shipped orders, but preferred to make the customer happy.

It turns out that there are a lot of Slammers in technical support and consumer call centers. These are the folks who want to spend as little time as possible on each call, and brag about first-contact resolution and short talk times. And it is true; your Slammers are probably your most productive employees. But at what cost? Remember, we are balancing quality, financial, and operational metrics, and while Slammers have high productivity, their quality isn't so good.

Common bad behavior from Slammers includes:

- **Hogging all the easy questions.** I saw this early on in my days as a support technician. One of my teammates went after every password reset or other simple question that came in, bragging about his productivity when he really was only answering fast, easy questions.

- **Dumping the caller as fast as possible.** When Slammers can't control their next call and they receive a complicated issue that requires a lot of work, they do whatever they can to get the customer off the phone as quickly as possible. When this happens, the customer usually calls back more irritated than ever because the issue is not resolved, and someone else has to deal with the problem.

- **Poor listening skills.** Slammers are so preoccupied with a fast resolution that they tend to focus on a symptom of the problem that they can easily fix instead of investigating what may be the root problem. Not only do they ignore extraneous details, but they don't document any of them in the incident, so the person following up afterward is unaware that additional critical information was offered but ignored.

Slammers, in general, have a short attention span. It isn't that they don't care about the customer or that they don't want to solve the problem. But because they are so predisposed to having an instant answer and not getting bogged down in details, sometimes they completely misread a situation and may even make a problem worse by applying a workaround or fix that doesn't address the root problem.

When coaching an employee with Slammer tendencies, be sure to stress the importance of a balanced performance, and be careful not to over-reward the Slammer's high productivity and ignore their low satisfaction scores. A workshop in active listening is a great idea to help the employee learn to ask all the right questions and document the findings before going into resolution mode.

The Geek

Having lived in Silicon Valley for more than 15 years, I certainly don't view the term "geek" as a pejorative. Extremely technical and intellectually curious, Geeks created Silicon Valley and continue to drive the innovation for which it is internationally known. As I've mentioned previously, technical skills are the single most valued trait for support analysts today, so it is no surprise that most technical support operations have a high percentage of Geek employees. While their technical prowess does lend itself to proficiency on the job, Geeks often have some secondary characteristics that are counterproductive, though monitoring and coaching can remedy the situation easily.

There are two common growth areas for Geeks, the first being a common Geek stereotype: good with technology, bad with people, and there definitely is some truth to that. I've certainly met many Geeks who were absolutely brilliant, but had zero people skills, to the point of being unintentionally rude and abrupt because conversation niceties were unknown to them.

An extreme case was a CRM developer that a good friend of mine married, much to the surprise of her friends who found her new fiancé rude to the point of being hostile, although he was clearly a brilliant engineer. I remember when they came back to visit after the birth of their first child. They were living in Canada, and I hadn't seen them since the wedding 2 years prior. I had a group of friends and former coworkers over for a cocktail party/baby shower, and when I threw the door open to greet the happy couple and their new baby, I was hit with a blistering tirade from The Geek about how he could figure out my phone number from the tones my condo building's ancient security system made when it dialed me. He said it was a pathetic, ridiculous design for a security entry system, and asked me why on earth I would live in a building with such shoddy security.

It certainly didn't get the party off to a very festive start or help assuage the lingering concerns we had that our friend had married a jerk.

But obviously not all Geeks are jerks. In fact, many Geeks—and, in general, the ones attracted to tech support roles—love technology and want to share it with you, bending over backward to explain things so customers can be enamored with the technology as well. Geeks have an air of confidence that lets customers know they are in good hands.

When interviewing a technical candidate, be sure to screen them for people skills. I like to ask them about their dream vacation or their favorite book or movie just to see how they communicate about nontechnology topics, as well as to identify some interest areas outside of technology. If the candidate only stops playing *World of Warcraft* long enough to go to work and rush back home, and his only vacation is Comic-Con once a year, maybe this isn't the right candidate for you.

There is one other problem area I have found with Geeks, and that is analysis paralysis. Being a logical, analytic thinker is a major strongpoint for most Geeks, but sometimes that trait goes too far.

I remember a Geek team manager I had who could drive me crazy. If you could fix a problem by doing a certain procedure 99 percent of the time, The Geek would start by doing what fixed the problem only 1 percent of the time "just to rule it out." He would come talk to me about some minor customer problem I had resolved, asking if I had checked all of this extraneous information that had nothing to do with the problem. Even though I had resolved the issue with the common procedure, he couldn't understand why we didn't try options B and C too, "just in case."

I don't know if this comes from a need to show off product knowledge or a fear of misdiagnosing a problem, but if you see high average talk times for your Geek employees, make sure they aren't overanalyzing every incident.

The Socialite

Depending on what personality test Socialites take, they will be classified along the lines of "amiable" or a "people person." This is an employee who values personal relationships over just about everything, meaning that they have terrific social skills, love interacting with customers, and are thrilled to solve a support problem because they know they are helping someone. I know I have a Socialite on the line when the agent asks, "How's the weather in Los Gatos today?"

I have a bias in favor of The Socialite, because as I've said previously, in the early days of technical support, agents were hired based on terrific social skills and technical aptitude, whereas today we tend to hire based on technical prowess and tolerate basic communication skills. If you want to use the Love the Customer philosophy with your support employees, Socialites will instantly understand and support the program.

While it is never safe to stereotype, in my opinion, Socialites make great employees because they genuinely want to please their manager and the customer, and they tend to appreciate coaching and constructive criticism. But that doesn't mean Socialites don't pose problems along the way.

The most common issue with Socialites is no surprise: They sometimes talk too much. This is actually where the name

"Socialite" comes from—by watching real socialites bounce from table to table at cocktail parties, making the rounds to see everyone. Technical support Socialites may do the same thing—when they finish a call or e-mail, they tend to wander around from cubicle to cubicle talking about the incident they just closed or engaging in general departmental gossip. This can become a real problem if The Socialite is interrupting other support techs, ultimately draining productivity. At one job, I actually gave an employee workshop on dealing with Socialites, recommending that as soon as they enter your workspace, you should grab a clipboard or legal pad and stand up, indicating you were about to leave. This usually is enough to keep all but the most dogged Socialite moving on to the next cubicle.

Because of the tendency to get carried away with conversations, Socialites may have longer-than-average talk times, so this is definitely something to keep an eye on. However, unless they talk to the point of wasting the customer's time, Socialites usually have high customer satisfaction scores because they come across as very friendly and engaged.

The other possible issue to consider with hiring Socialites is technical aptitude. While I do believe that most people are capable of learning technology and how to support it, Socialites may not be wired for problem solving and analysis in the same way as a degreed engineer. It doesn't mean that they can't learn this behavior, but it is something you should screen for during interviews and definitely address during training, such as diagnostic techniques and problem identification steps.

The Creative

Back in the 1990s, many of the big management gurus, such as Tom Peters, had a common theme: Hire the "weird" candidate. The technology industry was starting to boom, America was becoming known for innovation more than manufacturing, and for the first time, companies were starting to push back at the image of Corporate America-cloned employees in navy blue two-piece suits, white shirts, and red power ties. Hiring managers were encouraged to look beyond the standard support technician profile and consider nontraditional candidates who would bring new ideas and new energy to the workplace.

This is certainly the case in the high-tech industry, particularly in development, and I've definitely had my share of coworkers with tie-dyed wardrobes, no shoes, Goth attire, head-to-toe tattoos, Mohawks and faux hawks, chanting meditators, poets, crazy cat ladies, van-living hippies, as well as degreed engineers who disappear over Highway 17 to Santa Cruz every time the surf's up—regardless of the project schedule.

The positive side of these employees, who I call Creatives, is that they question the status quo, force you to rethink standard operating procedures, and offer a steady stream of alternate approaches, new ideas, and different views on just about everything. This left-brain thinking is definitely at the root of many product and process innovations, as long as you remain open to new ways of thinking.

The downside of Creatives is that they can needlessly complicate even the simplest process or program, and their insistence on thinking differently can sometimes come across as a refusal to follow protocol. I've managed a number of Creatives who were always ready to go "win-lose" on any topic, absolutely refusing to cooperate or participate, even though their reasoning seemed very minor or even petty to me.

As big a pain in the ass as Creatives can be, their input forces you to challenge assumptions and the status quo, so groupthink (or blindly following arbitrary decisions because no one expresses an alternate view) doesn't happen.

Creatives may not have perfect people skills, and some Creatives share a tendency toward intellectual snobbery with their Geek peers. When interviewing a Creative, be sure to test for patience and the ability to do repetitive work without becoming bored.

Provided they have good soft skills, customers tend to love Creatives, who manage to get to the answer using nontraditional lines of questioning or diagnostics. The most likely of any of the four employee types to be at genius level, Creatives see patterns and associations in customer problems that the rest of us overlook, enabling them to sometimes shortcut problem diagnostics, reduce resolution time, and increase first-contact resolution.

Back in my POS support days, I remember a JCPenney store that had their entire retail platform go off-line, and it took a day of downtime to isolate a failing power supply, which hadn't given any indication it was beginning to fail. A few weeks later, the same store had their system fail again—an extreme rarity—and again, it took a day to isolate another failed power supply. A few weeks later, the power supply failed for the third time.

While most of us were at a loss, The Creative on the team heard the repair representative mention that he was late arriving to the appointment because of heavy rain, and The Creative remembered seeing something in one of the previous incidents mentioning rain. It turned out that there was moisture wicking its way into the wall behind the POS equipment, so every time there was heavy rain, there was enough moisture leaking into the room to knock out the power supply, but not enough to cause a puddle or otherwise indicate that water damage was the problem.

The Creative solved the problem by free association and looking for a nontraditional root cause.

When managing Creatives, be mindful that their creative tendencies may make them push back at less glamorous parts of the job, such as detailed documenting of incidents and solutions, and sometimes their communication skills with coworkers need a bit of polish. As independent thinkers, Creatives are great for special projects requiring creativity—especially new technology projects, since Creatives tend to question existing procedures—making sure you don't reimplement a process that isn't currently working well.

Putting It All Together: Employee Types and Metrics Management

To properly manage support employees, managers need to combine their management skills with metrics management, and in this section, I wanted to merge the learnings from this and the previous chapter with some final recommendations. If you have a good understanding of the strengths and weaknesses of each employee, and you also have a good grasp on what drives each metric and how metrics interrelate, you should be able to analyze performance metrics with a much more knowing eye.

For an example, I'm using three different metrics:

- **Customer satisfaction, or CSAT.** For this example, I'm using a five-point scale, with five representing "highly satisfied" and one representing "highly unsatisfied." According to the TSIA Support Services Benchmark, the average satisfaction score for "overall interaction" for phone incidents and company-owned employees (as opposed to outsourced workers) is 4.39. For my example, I'm using a target CSAT score of 4.0.

- **Average talk time.** While talk times for high-volume, low-complexity consumer contact centers may be short—under 10 minutes—average times for enterprise support calls are longer, currently at 19.3 minutes for inbound customer calls handled by company-owned employees. For this example, I'm using a target talk time of 20 minutes.

- **First-contact resolution, or FCR.** Clearly, the less complex the technology being supported, the higher the FCR, with large enterprise software and hardware deployments often too complex for a problem to be identified—let alone resolved—on the first interaction. The current average FCR for enterprise firms is 53.08 percent. For this example, I'm using a target FCR of 60 percent.

With a good handle on each employee's personality and work style, a manager can interpret metrics to help identify employee types (*Figure 1.3.2*). As an example:

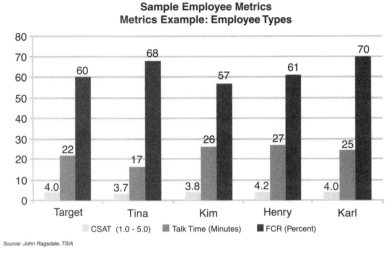

Sample Employee Metrics
Metrics Example: Employee Types

Source: John Ragsdale, TSIA

Figure 1.3.2: Sample Employee Metrics

- **Tina.** Tina's very low talk time and very high FCR indicate she may be a Slammer. Her slightly lower-than-average CSAT score indicates customers may feel rushed, but it isn't low enough to show she is cutting them off without solving their problem. As a manager, I would listen to some of Tina's calls to see if she allows customers to ask all of their questions and that they fully understand the resolution before the call is disconnected.

- **Kim.** Kim's low FCR, coupled with higher-than-average talk time, is a pattern you often see with new employees. However, knowing Kim's technical expertise, these numbers indicate that she is exhibiting Geek behavior, overanalyzing situations to be certain of the solution. Kim's lower-than-average CSAT score may mean she is frustrating customers with too many questions and repeating diagnostic steps. As Kim's manager, I would review her individual incidents and resolution time to be sure she isn't overcomplicating problems and verify that she is trying the most common solution first, every time.

- **Henry.** Henry has the highest CSAT score on the team, so clearly customers like working with him. However, Henry's talk time is also the highest on the team, indicating Henry is overcommunicating with customers and is probably a Socialite. The FCR numbers indicate Henry is being effective, so as Henry's manager, I would coach him on techniques for closing out a call on a friendly note, without further extending talk time.

- **Karl.** The final member of the team, Karl, has incredibly high FCR, but his talk-time numbers are only slightly above average, so he isn't spending too much time analyzing each incident. Instead, Karl seems to be uncovering clues and making connections more quickly than average employees, indicating he is a Creative. Karl's good CSAT score indicates customers are satisfied with the results, so as Karl's manager, I would spend time understanding Karl's diagnostic processes to see if he has uncovered some secrets from which other support techs could benefit.

« Key Lessons Learned from Chapter 3 »

Managing a support team with many different personality types and added stress from customers in crisis is very challenging. I've been surprised many times at how companies will have such mature training classes for new support technicians, but new managers are thrown to the wolves and told to figure it out on their own. One of my goals in writing this book was that these first three chapters could serve as a training manual for new support managers. Here is a recap of some key lessons learned regarding managing employees from this chapter:

- **Great support techs don't necessarily make great support managers.** While most great support managers started as frontline agents, that doesn't mean every good agent will make a good manager. Screen management candidates for organizational skills, ability to work with different kinds of people, patience, and ability to see the big picture.

- **Avoid promoting a team member to manage their existing team.** Moving from an individual contributor to a manager provides plenty of challenges for an employee; don't create more by promoting the employee to manage the group he worked in for a long period of time. Being a coworker one day and a manager the next day may be hard for the new manager, but it will be even harder for his teammates.

- **Treat employees as individuals.** Managers must be able to interact with each employee uniquely, depending on their personality, sense of humor, educational level, etc. Don't assume that what works with one employee will work with another, including your approach to coaching and offering constructive criticism.

- **Use performance metrics as indicators of employee performance.** Managers tend to use metrics to identify workers who are way above or below a goal or target, but looking closer at the numbers, including differences within the acceptable range, will give clues to each employee's style and habits. Talk times can indicate being too talkative or too abrupt; first-contact resolution rates can indicate technical aptitude or lack of diagnostic skills.

TALES FROM THE VAULT: A LESSON UNLEARNED

"Dammit, sir," Judge Stevens said, "will you accuse a lady to her face of smelling bad?"

—William Faulkner, *A Rose for Emily*

JCPenney is known for providing excellent management training, and the basics I learned there—such as simple scripts for counseling employees, disciplinary action, and if necessary, termination conversations—I still use today. While the formal approach to dealing with employees will always keep your actions documented and legal, over the years I've had to unlearn some of that formality. Here's an example, using a fairly common but never discussed Silicon Valley high-tech problem.

California's Bay Area has one of the most diverse populations in the U.S., and when you cram that many cultures into a tight warren of cubicles, mishaps do occur. Early in my Silicon Valley days, I received multiple complaints that one of my employees had an odor problem. This came as no surprise to me, because when I had closed-door meetings with this employee, I feared the paint would peel off the walls.

Following my JCPenney management training, with HR involved, I did a formal counseling session with the employee, clearly explained the situation, and asked for his help in a resolution. A full report of the conversation was duly placed in the employee's file. I followed my "best practice," and the problem was solved, but I was embarrassed and uncomfortable, and so was the employee.

A few years later, the same thing happened again. A project manager came to me because one of my employee's body odor was so strong that the manager had stopped inviting him to meetings. A few trips past his cubicle let me know the manager wasn't exaggerating. Instead of scheduling a formal meeting, I grabbed the employee on his way back from lunch, and very casually explained that Americans have a lot of crazy hang-ups, and one of them is that we don't think people should smell like people. I asked him to please humor me, take a shower before work each day, consider using deodorant, and he would never have to worry about offending our delicate American sensibilities.

The problem was solved, but this time, neither of us was uncomfortable, and, in fact, we joked about it later.

If you love your employees, you would never counsel them about an issue in such a way as to cause embarrassment. And managers need to learn when formal processes are best, and when a friendly aside can accomplish as much or more.

Section 2

The Vendor Years

IF EVER THERE WAS A CRAZY TIME TO MOVE TO SAN JOSE, THE capital of California's Silicon Valley, it was 1995. The initial public offering (IPO) boom with technology start-ups was just gearing up, and semiconductors and mainframe tools were king. There was an energy back then that everyone in high-tech companies felt, and hard workers were receiving big payoffs with stock options and four- and five-figure bonuses. I worked a lot of weekends and slept under my desk more than once, and so did everyone else.

Growing up in a Midwestern farming community, I had never been exposed to much wealth, and as exciting as Silicon Valley was, it was also obnoxious to go to lunch and hear people at the tables around you discussing how much they were worth "on paper" at that precise moment. Companies were handing out stock options like Halloween candy, and stock splits happened all the time, doubling or tripling your prospects.

When it came to making money from stock, my timing was always lousy. My first start-up was sold after I signed my employment agreement but before I reported to work, so I had zero vested shares and didn't make a cent from the acquisition. My next high-tech employer had gone public a few months before I joined, so many of my coworkers were worth millions of dollars, but I never earned enough stock money for anything other than a few nice vacations.

On three occasions, the Silicon Valley company I worked for had been acquired by a larger firm, but after receiving the initial chunk of retention stock they grant you to dissuade you from leaving, the golden spigot turns off, with subsequent options granted at such a high strike price I could never make much of a profit from selling them.

The technology industry, and Silicon Valley, has certainly changed a lot since 1995. Those huge boom years were followed by a decade of layoffs, partial economic recoveries, and then even more downturns, and you don't hear about people sleeping under their desks anymore. Not only has the energy level of the industry trailed off, but with stock options harder to come by and matching 401K programs all but forgotten—as well as the knowledge that your "at will" employer will eliminate your job at a moment's notice with no regret or severance pay—job security and employee loyalty have evaporated.

The role of technical support analyst has also changed a lot since 1995. To begin with, everyone knows what a support technician is today, thanks largely to the massive offshore outsourcing of support in 2002 that delivered such horrible customer experiences that just about every consumer in North America now understands "accent neutralization." Maybe the outsourcing rush gave our industry a black eye, but it certainly raised our visibility, and it also marked the beginning of the shift from cost center to profit center. For the first time, customers understood how inconvenient bad service could be, and suddenly they were willing to pay more for better service.

Outsourcing of contact center and technical support jobs continues, with new offshore areas growing in popularity all the time. Current hot spots include new areas within Asia (Singapore, the Philippines), Latin America (Nicaragua, Brazil), and Eastern Europe (Czech Republic, the Baltic states). However, with the

U.S. economy in decline and labor costs dropping, outsourcing centers are becoming common in some lower-wage areas of the U.S., such as Kansas and Utah, and "onshoring" efforts to pull some offshore traffic back onshore are common.

Another big change to the support industry over the last decade is compensation. Back in the start-up days, tech support analysts worked insane hours, doing whatever it took to keep customers running. Support employees were largely salaried (or exempt) workers with no overtime pay.

The United States Fair Labor Standards Act (FLSA), which governs labor practices in the U.S., states that some computer systems analysts, computer programmers, and software engineers who meet certain tests regarding their job duties are eligible for exempt status. A casual reading of these "tests" may lead support management to assume this exemption applies to technical support roles. However, a Department of Labor ruling dated December 4, 1998 (BNA, WHM 99:8201), declared that this exemption does not include employees who "provide technical support for business users by loading and implementing programs to businesses' computer networks, educating employees on how to use the programs, and by aiding them in troubleshooting."

FLSA does classify managers as exempt, but to qualify for the exemption, employees must spend more than 50 percent of their time performing management functions. In support environments, team leads or shift managers who continue to handle customer issues in addition to supervisory functions may have difficulty documenting the time spent performing managerial work to prove the exemption is warranted.

In the past few years, multiple high-tech companies have been hit with employee class-action lawsuits asking for unpaid overtime wages for support technicians incorrectly classified as exempt. In 2006, IBM agreed to pay $65 million to settle a federal class-action suit on behalf of 32,000 employees, and most recently, Oracle agreed to pay $35 million to settle a California class-action lawsuit with about 1,725 support, quality assurance, and project management employees in November 2011.

When employees win the suits, not only are companies forced to pay back wages to them, but also to reclassify positions as non-exempt and make adjustments to employee base pay. Unfortunately, the employees are often left unsatisfied with the final result, as the adjustments to base salary could mean as much as a 30 percent drop in pay. Other companies have quietly transitioned employees from exempt to nonexempt status to avoid legal action.[1,2]

In my opinion, the single biggest change to contact centers and technical support has been the impact of technology. When I started as a support representative, creating a support incident using our mainframe IBM Infosys system could take 3 to 5 minutes, with painful response-time delays up to a minute every time you pressed a PF key. There were no knowledgebases—just shelves and shelves and shelves of manuals, exploding with yellow sticky notes. There was no web self-service, no online communities, no Google. The only channel was phone—we didn't even have voice mail back then.

While all of the technology we enjoy today has dramatically impacted productivity, as well as introducing self-service to deflect assisted support interactions, successfully selecting and implementing support technology is not easy. The chapters in this section will focus on picking the right tool and tips to roll it out with the least drama and the highest adoption by employees and customers.

4 | Knowledge Management

As a technology analyst, I answer questions for companies in my area of expertise. Though I cover a lot of technologies, operational metrics, and best practices, there is one area that always consumes the lion's share of inquiries: knowledge management (KM) for support. In fact, over the last year, 31 percent of the inquiries I received from TSIA members were related to knowledge management, search, and web self-service. The second category, at 24 percent, was CRM and incident management.

I am very passionate about knowledge management because of my personal experience with technology revolutionizing the way we supported customers at JCPenney, and I've seen knowledge management or knowledgebases (KB) do the same for many other companies. In fact, I've often said that KM is one of the few support technologies in which you will receive 100 percent ROI for the project, even if you do a poor job of implementing it. True, ROI may take 18 months instead of 6, but the potential for KM is so huge that even a mediocre implementation can create large impacts.

The impact of a knowledge management implementation on support technician or contact center agent productivity is wide-reaching, as many productivity metrics are linked. When evaluating the return on investment of knowledge management in terms of agent productivity, here are the key metrics to monitor:

- **Average talk/handling time.** Before knowledgebases, support engineers relied on a library of binders with product and problem information, and most tech workstations were covered with yellow sticky notes with reminders and late-breaking information. The time taken to identify a needed piece of information could be quite long, stretching out the average talk time and average incident-handling time of each customer problem. By placing all KB information at the fingertips of the agent, techs can find any piece of information instantly, drastically lowering phone time with customers and reducing overall resolution time for incidents.

- **First-contact resolution (FCR) rate.** With information easily and quickly available to support techs, more issues can be resolved on the first interaction since customers no longer need to be placed on hold or called back later while the agent researches the issue using paper manuals, reads case histories from previous incidents, or discusses the issue with his or her supervisor or peers. FCR is also a primary driver of customer satisfaction.

- **Incidents handled per shift.** As average incident-handling time decreases and first-contact resolution increases, agents are able to handle more incidents per shift, allowing the same volume of inbound interactions to be handled by fewer technicians.

- **Training days per year.** Support engineer training has changed dramatically over the last decade. Not only have training methods changed as younger workers tend to find e-learning (prerecorded sessions delivered to the employee desktop) more effective than classroom training, but also mature knowledgebases of content mean agents need to be trained only on the basics, not on how to handle every conceivable problem they will encounter. Companies have seen training time reduced with the introduction of searchable knowledge repositories, with new hires "going live" faster than in the past, and experienced agents spending less time off the phone attending training.

As seen in *Figure 2.4.1*, support technicians spend 3 or more weeks a year in technical and customer service skills training. With technology complexity increasing, knowledgebases help support employees be experts on any topic, without additional off-phone training time.

But knowledge management isn't just about increasing productivity or trying to deflect more questions to web self-service. There are two other enormous benefits to an effective KM program that no one ever talks about: putting a price on problems and prioritizing bugs and enhancements.

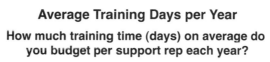

Average Training Days per Year

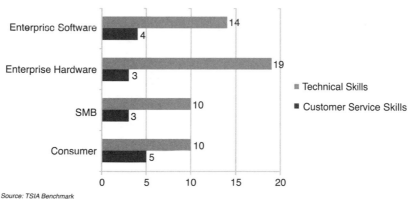

Figure 2.4.1: Average Training Days per Year

The ROI of KM: Beyond Productivity Improvements

While companies implement KM tools primarily to cut costs, I think the greater benefit of a strong KM program is the analysis it allows you to perform on what questions people are asking and how much it costs to support them. Armed with this information, you can force some changes to the organization that may not have been possible before. Let me explain.

At the core of the knowledgebase is the ability to link any knowledgebase article or articles to any support incident, and to link any support incident to any knowledgebase article or articles. In database terms, this is a many-to-many (M2M) relationship, meaning many incident records can be linked to many KB articles. With these links in place, companies can finally begin to accurately count how many times each problem or error situation occurs, determine who is encountering each problem, and perform root cause analysis about issues. You can immediately see if a problem is more prevalent with a specific version, geography, vertical industry, or other parameter.

To calculate how much it is costing you to support a particular problem, multiply the number of incidents of a problem, bug, or enhancement request, times the average resolution time for the problem, times the average cost per minute for the support center. (Average cost per minute is derived by adding all operational costs including payroll and overhead, and then dividing by the total number of incident resolution minutes for the time period.) I call this "calculating the cost of doing nothing." In other words, what will it cost my support organization to continue to resolve this problem for customers? Or, how much could we save by fixing the root cause?

The same approach can be used to help prioritize bugs and enhancements for future releases. My experience is that while technical support is on the front line with customers, we typically have much less influence to push for bug fixes than product management, development, or sales. To help change this, start calculating what it costs you to support common bugs and enhancement requests. Armed with those numbers, you will have much more negotiating power. Additionally, if development needs to research a fix, you have a record of every customer who has encountered the problem, what version they are using, and how or when the error occurred.

Ensuring Success: Common Reasons for KM Program Failure

In upcoming chapters, I will talk about common reasons that technology projects fail. But in addition to those overarching reasons, this section will discuss three critical issues specific to knowledge management projects. From the number of complaints I receive about these three problems, I'm guessing every support operation struggles with them to some degree.

Lack of Employee Participation

This is a problem everyone encounters: Some employees are reticent to contribute their knowledge to the system because they fear it will make them less valuable. To get reluctant employees on board, it certainly helps if the push to contribute comes from above, so all employees know the program has executive support.

Ultimately, knowledgebase contributions are best encouraged through a manager's two best tools: the carrot and the stick. The carrot means rewards, and the stick means the threat of punishment. Employees tend to prioritize activities that are clearly linked to performance reviews, bonuses, and raises, so if knowledgebase contributions are highly valued in the employee review and recognition process, most employees will participate.

The alternative is the stick, meaning employees who do not contribute, or who regularly contribute garbage, must receive some sort of disciplinary action, typically a lower score on their performance review, which impacts raises and bonuses. But beyond these basic employer avenues, here are some other hints.

- **From drudgery to challenging.** Many people who don't want to contribute to your knowledge efforts are coming from a place of insecurity. They've worked hard for their knowledge, and they fear that if they share it with everyone, they will no longer be valuable. As a manager, I could usually solve this easily by coaching them that documenting their knowledge means someone else can now solve those redundant issues, leaving the employee to work on more interesting and challenging problems.

- **Sell them on the ROI.** One of the biggest employee complaints about new technology is that it is "shoved down our throats." Be sure everyone is on board with the KM project *before* it goes live. Let employees sit in on demos and participate in beta tests. If they understand the value of KM to the organization and how the tool improves performance *and* makes the support tech an expert on every problem, it is easier to get them on board and participating.

- **Learn from high achievers.** When you identify top contributors to the knowledgebase, don't just reward the high achievers; share their secrets. Have them talk at staff meetings about how they write articles, give examples of good and bad articles, and use analytics to show the impact of good knowledge (linked to solved incidents, for example). Be sure you have good editors in place, and templates that make writing easy, even for those who find writing to be a chore.

Lack of Customer Adoption

Simply put, if customers don't use your web self-service tools, you will never receive a return on your investment. Having a big launch with incentives to use the system is important, and touting early victories (like improvements in first-contact resolution or resolution time) to everyone is a great way to highlight the benefits of the system. Studies have shown that if customers have a poor experience using your self-service site, they may never try again. So if you do make improvements, you're going to have to sing it from the rafters.

In general, boosting adoption of customer self-service requires a healthy dose of marketing—not a skill most support operations are known for. Involve your marketing department and include messaging about available self-service resources in as many customer touch points as possible. Have recordings remind customers of self-service while they are on hold for a phone agent. Include links to self-service in every e-mail, bill, print advertisement, and any other customer communication. Have booths to promote self-service at all user events and conferences. Include self-service promotions in every customer training class and manual. Publish brief case studies showing how customers are using self-service, especially when new features are introduced.

Lack of Maintenance

Knowledge management initiatives are launched with the best of intentions. New technology is introduced, new processes for capturing and publishing content are rolled out, employees are given incentives to contribute knowledge articles, and customers are encouraged to access new online knowledge tools. Within 2 to 3 months, positive business results are realized. With accurate knowledge at their fingertips, support technicians are able to resolve issues faster, reducing average handle time and increasing first-contact resolution rates. Customers find that the new online content is extremely helpful, and adoption and success of self-service rises, reducing assisted support calls. Everyone's happy.

Then something changes. The knowledge project is de-emphasized, resources are moved to other projects, little new content is created, and existing content grows stale. Within a couple of years, the formerly popular, dynamic, and cost-effective knowledgebase has become an obstacle, and both employee and customer satisfaction suffer as a result. Metrics such as first-contact resolution and average incident-handling time that improved a year earlier begin to reverse, and as new products and versions are released to customers with little or no associated knowledge content created, operational metrics begin a slow decline.

Why are popular and successful knowledge management programs left to flounder and ultimately fail? There are three common denominators for de-emphasized KM programs:

1. **Project funding is reduced after go-live.** A common reason cited for the lack of ongoing maintenance, and ultimately a failing KM program, is that project funding is eliminated or severely reduced. After the initial launch excitement wanes and early metric increases begin leveling off, other projects become higher priorities, and staff dedicated to the KM program are pulled off and assigned to new projects. While it is true that knowledge management projects need additional resources up front, it is critical that when creating the budget for a project, funding for ongoing content resources are guaranteed for the life of the project. If executives will not commit to long-term dedicated resources—whether those are specific people or full-time equivalents across a group of employees—the likelihood for failure is high.

2. **Loss of a project champion.** Another reason cited for declining knowledge management programs is the loss of the project champion. KM initiatives are often pet projects led by a supervisor or manager with a passion for the topic, and likely these project owners have experience implementing knowledgebases for other companies. If the project champion leaves the company or is assigned to another department or project, there is no one left to rally the troops. Interest in the project fades, and work to create and maintain content ends. When launching a new KM initiative, be sure to designate multiple project leads, spreading ownership of the program across multiple people, so that losing any one individual will not stop a project.

3. **Lack of insight.** Another common problem that can lead to inadequate content maintenance and declining KM success is a lack of insight into the success of the initiative due to having no analytics to help understand consumption trends and missing content. Companies using older knowledge tools, or those that leverage a general-purpose data warehouse instead of a platform specifically designed for technical support knowledge management, are missing the analytics included in best-of-breed products that not only help track ROI for the project, but also allow sophisticated reporting on content consumption trends and even pinpoint missing content.

As complicated as it may be to create and maintain highly successful knowledge management practices, there are some companies that have it all figured out. A great example of a company that has successfully embedded knowledge management best practices into their core operation is TSIA member VMware, the fifth-largest infrastructure software company in the world.

At VMware, knowledge management is included in core support engineer training from Day One. New hires receive KM best-practice training as part of onboarding, and are equipped with the skills to begin contributing to the knowledgebase from the very beginning. Contributions to the knowledgebase are required in order to progress up the career ladder, with top contributors receiving awards and recognition. High-performing KM contributors are considered for a Knowledge Champion role, a 6-month rotation focusing solely on knowledge creation, editing, and maintenance.

Not only is knowledge core to the support operation, but customer self-service is thriving. With over 10 million web self-service sessions a year, customers consider VMware's knowledge team to be rock stars. They are asked to present at user conferences on top support issues and to share tips and tricks for leveraging the online tools.

"By developing and implementing a best-in-class knowledge management social media strategy, we've been able to proactively deliver timely, relevant technical support information to our customers, helping them maintain optimal performance of their virtualization and cloud infrastructures," says Scott Bajtos, senior vice president, Global Support Services and Customer Advocacy, VMware. "Our innovative knowledge management social media strategy has not only improved our customer support experience, it has also helped our organization deflect support cases."

« Key Lessons Learned from Chapter 4 »

Knowledge management is one of the mostly widely adopted technologies by support organizations. With the rising complexity of today's hardware and software, support employees and customers can't possibly remember everything about the products and need some central repository of problem resolution scenarios to access when problems arise. Some key takeaways from this chapter are:

- **KM impacts on employee productivity.** Knowledge management projects can have a big impact on employee productivity, with positive changes to the following metrics: average talk/handling time, first-contact resolution rate, incidents handled per shift, and number of training days per year.

- **Other business impacts of KM.** By linking every customer incident to a knowledgebase article or articles, reporting on what customers are calling about is straightforward. Additionally, you can easily mine this data in order to understand which customer demographics (location, size of company, product version) are experiencing certain problems and to help prioritize bugs and features for an upcoming release.

- **Why KM programs fail.** While usually even mediocre knowledge projects have a positive business impact, when KM programs fail, it usually is due to one of three reasons.

    1. Lack of employee adoption is a success killer, because if no one contributes new articles or uses existing content, the project generates no value.

    2. Lack of customer adoption is another common problem, as companies hope to cut costs by deflecting assisted support interactions to self-service, but if customers never use the self-service system, no incidents are deflected.

3. Lack of maintenance is the third common reason for KM project failure. Knowledge must be frequently updated to keep content current and accurate and to always improve readability and consumption. Without ongoing maintenance, articles become stale, and both employees and customers stop using the system.

TALES FROM THE VAULT: ANALYTICS' ROLE IN KNOWLEDGE MANAGEMENT

With the massive amount of data available about how employees and customers interact with knowledge, we are just now uncovering the tip of the iceberg about the sophisticated reporting and analytics for knowledge management. There are a few companies already rolling up their sleeves and launching programs to mine knowledge usage data in order to improve operational efficiency and the customer experience.

A great example comes from a TSIA member, a large global independent software company serving 99 percent of the Fortune 1000. The company's enterprise support team has more than 2,000 employees around the globe, handling more than half a million support incidents per year—more than half of which are resolved the same day.

With the critical nature of the firm's support issues, which relate to technology security, the company launched an initiative to evaluate all of the customer support touch points, including analyzing their annual volume of assisted support incidents, millions of self-service transactions, and millions more discussion forum posts and views, to better understand emerging key performance indicators (KPIs) and create an analysis framework to identify top content.

One of the first steps was identifying what could be measured, and the company identified four sources of information to assist in the project: their content management system (CMS), which tracks article views and customer clickstreams; their intelligent search platform, which tracks search rankings of content and content e-mailed to others by customers; their community platform, which tracks feedback on posted articles and whether customer discussion threads are resolved; and their CRM/incident management system, which tracks the number of times articles are linked to closed incidents.

With KPIs identified, the firm created an Article Value Index (AVI), a customer-focused analytical methodology that determines an individual knowledge article value score relative to a calculation based on direct customer feedback, direct customer interaction with the knowledge article, and customer session activity. Direct customer feedback metrics include "helpful/not helpful" prompts and forum posts marked "closed with an article." Metrics related to direct customer interaction with the article include article views, bookmarked articles, and articles viewed for more than 60 seconds or less than 30 seconds. Average customer session activity includes metrics such as average number of clicks to access an article and average number of clicks from search results.

With all of the metrics identified and loaded into a data warehouse, analysis could begin. A relative weight was assigned to each metric to use in calculations, with metrics the project team considered most important given a higher weight. Then, the AVI could run, evaluating every piece of content in the knowledgebase and online community, identifying the most useful content as well as poor content, which could be flagged for editing or removal.

The project began by analyzing the top 500 most-viewed articles for a single product and found validation: There was a substantial relationship between an article's AVI score and how it tracked against page-view or case-linking ranking. In fact, a third of the articles with the highest AVI score accounted for over half of all page views and over 60 percent of all incident links.

Now that the company is able to automatically identify the most actionable content on their website, they are giving top articles prominent placement on high-traffic support landing and community pages to further raise visibility for useful content and shortcut self-service.

5 | Selecting Technology

THE PRIMARY WAY COMPANIES SELECT ENTERPRISE TECHNOLOGY today is via the request for proposal (RFP) process. The company creates an RFP document listing hundreds—and unfortunately, I've seen thousands—of requirements. Exhaustive laundry lists of functionality, including features every single product on the market already has, and usually, a multitude of features the company would never use in a million years. The thinking is that if the vendors will all fill out the RFP, then all we have to do is add up the check marks and pick the best product, right?

Wrong. I've worked for vendors, and I've responded to RFPs. Do you really think a vendor is going to answer no to any required feature if they think it will impact their ability to close the deal? No way. As one of my marketing mentors was fond of saying, marketing isn't about black and white or yes and no; marketing is all about the gray areas. And with enough mental creativity, I found I could answer yes to just about every RFP requirement, whether it was "out of the box" in my product or not.

To make matters worse, many publicly available RFP templates are created by vendors, slanting every requirement question in such a way as to make their solutions look stronger than their competitors'. Picking a product by tallying votes on an RFP means you have accepted marketing-speak as gospel, and project success is about as likely as meeting and marrying Prince Charming on your next day trip to Disneyland. The RFP process is fantasyland.

Here is the five-step process I recommend companies use to select enterprise technology. The focus is on solving business problems, not on creating laundry lists of features. Remember, you are seeking a collaborative relationship with the vendor, not an adversarial one.

Five-Step Process for Selecting Enterprise Technology

1. Define business goals for the project.
2. Identify a short list of "best-fit" vendors.
3. Ask vendors for references with similar business results.
4. Arrange a "customized demo" for vendor finalists.
5. Identify the winning vendor.

Each of these steps is described in detail in the following sections.

Step One: Define Business Goals for the Project

I think this is the most important step of the project, but unfortunately, it is a step many companies miss. You are implementing this technology for a reason, so get your goals and expectations right out there on the table. This is an easy way to quickly find out which vendors can meet your business needs and which vendors don't belong on the short list.

What metrics do you expect the project to impact, and by how much? List them, along with your current average for each metric and your intended goal. Examples include: "Improve first-contact resolution from 42 percent to 60 percent" or "Improve transactional CSAT average from 4.1 to 4.4 or higher." All metrics are game, from across operational, financial, and quality categories.

How do you know which metrics will be impacted and how much improvement to expect? Ideally, you've done this homework already by talking to industry peers, reading case studies, and interviewing industry analysts, like me, who can give you specific examples, provide input on realistic improvement ranges, and line up peers to talk to who have gone through similar projects. Over the years I've published many research reports about the ROI for technology, listing specific metrics that are impacted by tools such as knowledge management, intelligent search, remote support, and online communities, along with case study examples.

Note that if you do this step correctly, you also will arrive at the budget for the project. By calculating the cost savings you will receive by achieving all of these metrics improvements, you should arrive at a total savings over 3 to 5 years from reduced head count, or additional volume from the same head count, improved margins, higher renewals, or other factors. The project budget should be tied to the expected business results of the project, so don't kick off a $2 million project if you only expect to receive $250,000 worth of business benefits.

Step Two: Identify a Short List of "Best-Fit" Vendors

One of my most frequent requests as a technology analyst is to help a company create a list of five or so "best-fit" vendors to identify for a potential technology project. I have my list based on what products I've seen other companies successfully use to resolve the same or comparable business problems on a similar scale as this company. The company also has a list, usually created by their IT department. And it is always at this point that a little song from my childhood, a *Sesame Street* classic, begins softly playing in my head:

> *One of these things is not like the others,*
> *One of these things just doesn't belong.*
> *Can you guess which thing is not like the others*
> *By the time I finish my song?*

I'm hearing this song in my head because invariably there is at least one—and usually more—vendor on the company's short list that simply doesn't belong. I've seen reporting vendors on lists of knowledge management projects. I've seen CRM vendors on the list for remote-control projects. I've seen back-office accounting vendors on the list for professional services automation (PSA) projects. I've seen it all. And when I gently ask, "I'm curious, how did Company X end up on this list?" the answer is always the same:

- "Our CEO is friends with their CEO."
- "Our vice president of sales plays golf with their vice president of sales."
- "Our CIO used to work there and thinks we can customize it to work."
- "Our venture capital backer also backs that company, and they want us to work together."

Now, I'm going to let you in on a little secret. Most areas of customer support technology are either mature or reaching maturity. For knowledge management and CRM, for example, *all* of the products out there are good, have referenceable customers, and will help you achieve your business goals. Pick any product on the "best-fit" list I provide and you can make a successful go of it, provided your processes are in order (see Chapter 6).

But if you want to be 100 percent certain your project fails, pick a vendor that doesn't even play in your industry because you have a social tie to the company. You will never achieve your intended business results. Your relationship with the vendor will sour, and you will be shopping for another product within 18 months.

If you are under pressure to pick a product that doesn't make sense because of some weird loyalty someone at your company has to the other company, just say no. If it is your CEO and you don't feel you can say no, then by all means try to find someone else to drive the project, because the project will end in defeat. When a technology project fails, it not only wastes valuable company resources, but it leaves a bad impression about that technology category with everyone in the operation, and the next project in this area will have even more employee and customer adoption challenges because of the early failure.

Just say no.

Step Three: Ask Vendors for References with Similar Business Results

When shopping for customer service technology, talking to each vendor's customer references is a critical step in making the right decision. During the sales cycle, it is very easy to get drawn into marketing messages and swayed by demonstrations of prototype products that are customized for each demonstration. Customer references are the only way to determine what functionality actually exists, how easy it is to implement, how the vendor supports its customer base, and how well it manages the overall relationship. This section outlines how to approach references and provides questions to ask when meeting with vendor references.

When the short list of vendors for a technology project is determined, it is time to start understanding what their products really have to offer, and a key step in evaluating each vendor is to utilize customer references. Below are some guidelines for managing the reference process and maximizing the effectiveness of each reference:

- **Focus on key capabilities.** Insist on references for any modules or functions that are critical for a successful implementation. Never accept reading a case study. You must talk to the customer(s) and understand how they are using the application. Verify that they are using the software to solve the same business problem you are experiencing in order to evaluate how well their experiences will apply to your environment. If you cannot talk to a customer using a key piece of functionality you need, assume it does not exist or is in a beta condition. Don't trust an untried application.

- **Define "out of box."** Ask about out-of-box functionality vs. site customization. What features or modules were they able to use with little or no customization? How much customization was involved? Were they able to do some or all of the customizations in-house, or was a consultant or systems integrator hired to perform the work?

- **Stick to your vertical.** Request references in your vertical market or industry. Modules that work perfectly for financial services may be inadequate for telecommunications. As an example, CRM systems designed for business-to-consumer (B2C) companies typically are missing the entitlement processes required for business-to-business (B2B) companies. Make certain there are reference companies that speak the same language to ensure there are no hidden "gotchas." Today, many software platforms are customized for each vertical market. If the vendor doesn't have experience in your industry, you will end up as a beta customer.

- **Stick to your platform.** Similarly, for on-premise technology, request references using your technology platform of choice. While functionality should be the same on all platforms, customers using less common configurations may wait months . . . or longer . . . for releases, and encounter stability or scalability problems not experienced by customers using the vendor's primary platform.

- **Go on-site.** While some phone references are fine, go to a few customer sites and talk to the people using the applications, as well as the frontline managers of the service teams. What do they think? What sort of training did the customer receive from the vendor? Were the system administrators provided with training free of charge? How many people have been to a formal training class held by the vendor, and what did they think of the content? What was end-user adoption like, and what do frontline workers think of the tool?

- **Ask the tough questions.** What worked and what didn't? What would you do differently next time? What was more difficult than promised? Ask the reference to give examples of problems encountered during implementation and how the vendor resolved the issues. Every implementation encounters challenges, and no product is perfect, so if the reference can only provide positive reports, ask specifically for the downside or consider the reference suspect.

- **Ask about "shelfware."** Did they implement all modules purchased? Is there a time line to implement any additional modules? Did they purchase any modules they never intended to implement?

- **Don't forget the "R" in CRM.** These vendors are selling service and relationship software; they should be the relationship experts. What sort of relationships do they have with the customers? Are the executives of both companies meeting periodically to discuss strategic direction? Does the vendor float product designs by customers for input? Do the customers have access to the product managers to talk about issues and enhancements? If the vendor does not truly manage relationships well, what is the chance its software will?

- **Go it alone.** Conduct all or part of the interview without the vendor present. Vendors often try to coordinate phone calls and site visits between customers and prospects, and the sales rep is included. Ask that they not be on the line for phone interviews. If they do accompany you on-site for a visit, request at least one meeting with key owners of the implementation with the vendor out of the room. There will be a freer flow of information without the vendor present.

- **Uncover payback schemes.** Finally, ask what the customer is getting in return for the reference. Though not as common today as during the technology boom years, some companies offer incentives and product discounts to customers for doing multiple references. Make certain that they're bragging about their successful implementation because it solved their business problems, not to get a free golf weekend or 200 free user licenses.

By following these guidelines, more useful information will result from reference calls and visits. Productive customer references will drive the purchase decision forward by confirming vendor claims, confirming concerns already present, or by raising new concerns the vendor must address before a sale can be made.

Step Four: Arrange a "Customized Demo" for Vendor Finalists

When you have narrowed the list down to a couple of vendors, the final step in the selection process is to arrange for an extended, customized demonstration. The vendor basically does a bare-bones implementation for you, allowing you to test the product. For on-demand products, the vendor will provide you with user logins to a test environment for evaluation. This is a critical point in the project selection phase, because now is a great time to involve all the employees who will ultimately use the tool.

Having a head-to-head "bake-off" is the best way to pick the right product, because you are receiving input from the intended end users who will be looking for ease of use and intuitive design. The more employees that can be involved in the extended test, the better, because they will be more likely to quickly adopt the product once implemented if they feel they had a hand in the selection. This step eliminates the common employee complaint that new technology is "shoved down their throats."

In years past, these customized demos, also known as "boardroom demos" or "proof of concepts," were a major expense for the vendor because they had to bring in all the necessary hardware, fly in consultants to implement the code and do the required customizations, as well as have sales and technical support available for any questions that arise. I remember nightmares trying to coordinate the delivery of big, bulky UNIX servers to prospects in New York and Minneapolis back in my start-up days.

The on-demand revolution has certainly simplified this process, as a software-as-a-service (SaaS) vendor can easily provision a fresh application instance and provide temporary user log-ons for customers who want to try out the package before buying it. In fact, I'd say the ability to try out SaaS applications for free has been one of the keys to on-demand adoption—salesforce.com offered free trials of their sales force automation (SFA) software from the very beginning, and it was a huge hit with sales teams right away.

Not only does the trial demo allow end users to try the applications and weigh in with their preference, but it also gives you a better idea how each vendor is to work with, the attitude of their consultants, how easy support is to access and work with, and how responsive development is to any problems that arise.

Step Five: Identify the Winning Vendor

At the end of the trial demonstration, selecting the winning vendor should be a simple decision. Collect feedback from all employees involved, being sure to pull from them specific reasons for their preference. In my experience, after evaluating how easy each vendor was to work with and which was more responsive to your needs, the final decision is obvious.

« Key Lessons Learned from Chapter 5 »

This chapter focused on a five-step process for selecting enterprise technology. The five steps are defining business goals for the project, identifying a short list of best-fit vendors, checking vendor references, arranging a customized demo for vendor finalists, and selecting the winning vendor. Key lessons learned from this chapter include:

- **The traditional RFP process is flawed.** This approach to selecting technology, which involves capturing hundreds of functional requirements and asking vendors to tally which ones they offer, allows the vendors too much creativity in answering yes to key requirements.

- **Start with metrics.** Each technology project is in response to a business need, so be clear about business goals for the project. Which specific metrics are you trying to improve, and by how much? Once you have this documented, identifying best-fit vendors is much easier.

- **Select possible vendors based on core competency and proven results.** Don't waste time on vendors with no history of success in this technology area or a company you have personal relationships with that doesn't really play in your market.

- **Ask the tough questions of vendor references.** Ask about ROI, implementation experience, how easy the vendor is to work with, and any hidden costs. Conduct at least part of the interview without the vendor present to be sure you are getting a straight answer, and consider making a site visit so you can talk with more users than just the system administrator.

- **A customized demo will build employee support for the project.** Have a "bake-off" of vendor finalists by having them provide a test implementation customized for your environment. Involve as many employees in the test as possible. Not only will their end-user perspective be important, but you are building excitement about the project and encouraging employee adoption of the new tool when it goes live.

**TALES FROM THE VAULT:
THE SALES REP DEFICIT**

Earlier I talked about how common it is to have a vendor on the short list that definitely doesn't belong there. But the opposite problem also happens regularly, and the root cause is the same every time.

Here's the scenario: I'm talking to a company about an upcoming technology project, trying to understand their goals for the implementation. It soon becomes obvious that a vendor who is a specialist in the problem the company is trying to solve is not on the short list, and instead, they are selecting from a group of vendors who all do something else. So I ask, "Um, why isn't Vendor X on the list?" And here is the universal reply: "Oh, we started with them, but their sales rep was a $#!@."

I don't think developers and marketers at high-tech companies have any idea how many deals they are losing based on the personality of the sales rep. What is really shocking is how many times the obvious best-fit vendor is dismissed from a deal because:

- The sales rep was arrogant (I've heard this a dozen times about certain vendors).

- The sales rep was late to multiple meetings or conference calls, and the company felt the vendor didn't want the business.

- The sales rep didn't know anything about product functionality and tried to bullshit his way through the meeting—always a big turnoff.

Sometimes I contact the vendor who has lost a particular deal in order to ask them about it. So far, not a single time has the win/loss report included anything about the sales rep or the sales process. Usually it is a useless excuse like, "They weren't ready to make a decision," when that obviously wasn't the case. Or, "We couldn't meet their price," when I knew the discussions never even got that far.

This is all very frustrating for me, because I want to see companies buy the right product to fix the right problem, and when there is a mismatch from Day One, it isn't good for any of us. The customer ultimately doesn't receive the ROI they expect. The vendor never has a referenceable customer. And I have far fewer success stories to write about than I should.

There is so much pressure in the service and support industry on satisfaction surveys, I wonder why companies aren't doing a better job of understanding the impression their sales staff is making on customers. Why doesn't the vice president of sales follow up with prospects after the initial sales visit to ask how it went? Why doesn't someone outside of sales create the win/loss reports so at least companies know how much business they are losing because of sales rep hubris?

For all of you in the enterprise support industry, ask yourself, "When was the last time I did a 'ride along' on a sales call?" Regardless of what your role is (engineering, support, or marketing), maybe you should start making your presence known in more customer-facing sales situations. From what I'm hearing, you may be shocked at what you see.

6 | Implementing Technology

THE SINGLE MOST IMPORTANT ELEMENT IN DETERMINING THE success of a new technology project is to ensure you have strong business processes in place. All of the innovative software bells and whistles in the world will not create business value if your underlying processes are broken. Whether you are able to refine and improve your processes on your own or you need to involve an expert consultant, service management must be sure that processes are documented, understood, and followed consistently before implementing new knowledge management, CRM, or other service-related tools.

Companies spend months—even years—creating the ideal request for proposal to identify best-fit technology for a new project, including exhaustive laundry lists of features. They do so with the belief that if they identify the most functionally rich product, their likelihood of long-term success is higher.

After many years of close involvement with technology projects, I now recognize that the most common reasons for project failure have less to do with the technology itself, and more to do with the company's business processes. This chapter will discuss common problems that thwart project success in hopes that companies planning to bring in new service and support tools will spend time up front on process refinement before launching a technology search. To begin, here are three hard-learned truths regarding process and technology:

- **Business process has more influence on project success than the tool selected.** In most areas of service and support technology, products are reaching maturity, and industry standards (IT Infrastructure Library, Knowledge-Centered Support) are creating more functional consistency across products. The truth is, you can have project success with most tools on the market. But if your groups can't communicate, if the data you capture isn't consistent across geographies, if escalation guidelines are constantly morphing, no product on the market can overcome your process problems.

- **Your company's processes are not that unique.** This comes as a major shock to most companies, who typically think their business problems, process flows, and organizational structures are so unique that they can't compare themselves to anyone else. After 2 dozen years helping companies tackle technology projects, I have found that companies are more alike than they are different. Incidents flow from an open state to a closed state; issues are escalated from one group to another group; information is collected and reports are generated. While each company may have different group names, different escalation parameters, unique products to support, and perhaps unique maintenance contract terms, support operations around the globe still have a great deal in common.

- **If you don't document your processes, you will pay someone to do it for you.** Let's face it: Documenting existing business processes is not a lot of fun. You must seek consensus on the correct workflow for every type of customer problem, including a few that have always been a bit gray. There will undoubtedly be some disagreements, some compromise, and a few problems uncovered along the way. But ultimately, if you don't have your processes documented, a consulting or professional services team will do it for you before any big technology project begins—and you will be paying them top dollar to do something you should have done yourself.

Top Two Reasons Technology Projects Fail

After a few years of down spending due to the economy, companies began shopping for new service and support technology again in 2010, and I expect the current buying binge to continue until 2015. Many support operations are struggling with decades-old CRM and knowledge management tools that are no longer under maintenance and impossible to integrate with newer tools. The popularity of on-demand tools is also causing companies to reevaluate their current technology infrastructure and look for more flexible and easy-to-maintain platforms.

It is critical that companies analyze their existing business processes and resolve conflicts prior to kicking off any new implementation. While every project failure may have some unique circumstances, I have identified two issues that are very often at the core of an unsuccessful technology deployment.

Automating Broken Processes

The first common reason for technology project failure is related to defective or broken processes. If a company has business processes that range from inadequate to completely broken, and instead of fixing them, they replicate them in the new tool, how is this going to fare in the long term? If your processes aren't working today, hard-coding them into a software platform will certainly not solve any problems.

A sure sign that a project is headed toward disaster due to bad processes is when project stakeholders defend themselves by saying, "But we've always done it that way!" Today's enterprise software packages include out-of-box workflows that are used by companies of all sizes. Many of the processes are based on industry standards. Before doing extensive modifications to best-of-breed tools, be sure to seek assistance from third-party process experts.

This is especially common in CRM and incident management. Many companies implementing CRM for the first time created custom account relationship models that don't allow forecast rollups, and defined automatic escalation rules for customer incidents without informing employees of the escalation guidelines. If there is no buy-in for the process, project go-live will be fraught with problems.

Here's a real-world example for you: A major North American communications firm implemented a new CRM system but did not receive the desired results. Incident resolution times were increasing, customer satisfaction scores were declining, and managers were having trouble pinpointing the root of the problem. I was brought in to evaluate the new CRM implementation and identify the problems. Here's what I found:

- Level 1 and Level 2 reported to different managers. These two managers hated each other. The animosity was obvious to everyone, and the employees adopted their managers' attitudes, not wanting to work with the other group. No amount of escalation rules seemed to work—Level 2 ignored issues coming from Level 1 because they didn't like them.

- Level 3 was a bigger problem. Level 3 consisted of individual employees in accounting who could fix customer billing records. These individuals were told by their manager that they were spending too much time on customer problems, and to limit their time doing Level 3 work to 30 minutes a day. So issues escalated to Level 3 sat ignored in the queue because the manager told employees the work was not a priority.

- Prior to the CRM project, customers would call Level 3 directly for some account issues. The Level 3 accounting experts didn't like that Level 1 was now trying to resolve some of those issues, so they refused to train Level 1 or author any knowledgebase articles about handling accounting issues, ensuring that Level 3 kept their internal designation as the "experts." Instead of off-loading common problems to Level 1, they kept them flowing to Level 3 . . . who refused to work the incidents.

In this scenario, the company had implemented logical work-flow routing and escalation rules, but because the employee groups had so much animosity toward each other and refused to communicate, no one played by the rules. Implementers had blindly hardcoded processes that were clearly not working and merely hoped for the best.

Implementing Technology in Lieu of Process

The second common reason for technology failure is almost the opposite of the first: Companies implement technology to provide process where none exists. This is especially common when companies are consolidating departments due to collapsing regions or because of corporate mergers and acquisitions. The consolidating departments have conflicting processes, and instead of doing the hard work to identify the right processes to use moving forward, the company implements a tool with generic processes and hopes the problems will go away.

Process problems never go away. When companies do not have defined business processes, everyone makes up their own, and getting everyone to move to consistent processes is a major change-management challenge. Software enables processes; it doesn't create them, and it certainly doesn't create consensus on processes. Employees who don't like the hard-coded processes will reject the tool and continue to do things the old way.

Documenting all processes, and ensuring that you have consensus on them, is critical before starting any new technology project. By the time the consultants are configuring the system, it is too late to start arguing process.

Here's another real-world example: A global insurance company was implementing a new CRM system for the southern region of their North American operation. I was on the team of consultants in charge of the project, and when we arrived, we found no process definitions and no agreement on how processes should be handled. We named the current workflow used by the company as "sneaker-net." When a customer called with a problem, the agent filled out a paper form with the problem details, and then a runner took the paper and ran across the corporate campus, dropping the paper off to whomever was the expert charged with fixing the problem.

The current system was pure chaos. Each runner had his or her own idea about who should handle what problem. Since the issues were tracked only on paper, many customer problems were forgotten when slips of paper were ignored or went missing. With no single view of incidents, customers calling for status updates received no news—or even assurance that someone was working on the problem.

After a very lengthy implementation project, every process was defined. The expert for every issue was documented and agreed upon; every expert was trained to work customer issues dispatched to their queue in the CRM system, and notification rules were set up to send e-mail notifications for new incidents to experts who didn't receive many tickets and weren't actively monitoring the queue. After months of drama and internal battles, we thought the company was ready to go live with new, defined, and logical processes.

When the first phone call came in on go-live day, instead of filling out a paper form, the agent dutifully filled out the ticket in the new CRM system. But, instead of forwarding the ticket to the correct queue, he printed it out and handed it to a runner, who took off across the campus to hand deliver the incident to the expert. We were flabbergasted and asked why, after months of process definition and employee training, had the company reverted to sneaker-net? It turns out they didn't know what to do with the employees hired as runners, so they decided to forget about automated processes and just keep on doing things the old way.

In the end, the company decided that offering poor customer service was better than embracing consistent, automated, auditable business processes.

It is critical that companies have their business processes in order prior to implementing new tools. This will help to ensure project success and maximum ROI for the implementation. Keep these recommendations in mind:

- **Start by documenting existing processes.** This is not a glamorous task, but a required one. Process documentation, using simple tools like Visio or one of the many "mind mapping" software packages now available, can be a great project for senior techs who can use their communications skills to help reach consensus across multiple groups and departments. Considering that professional services consultants charge an average of $100 to $200 per hour, if you don't document your own processes, be prepared to pay your vendor's project team $30,000 to $70,000 for two to three consultants for a few weeks of process documentation.

- **Be cautious when veering away from "out of box."** Unique business processes may definitely be a competitive differentiator, or you may have an innovative approach to an old problem. But before spending significantly to replicate a nonstandard process into a software platform, evaluate the out-of-box process and be sure your unique approach is delivering value. Don't be different just for the sake of being different, unless it delivers value to the organization.

- **Benchmarking is a good way to identify good and bad processes.** TSIA manages benchmark surveys across multiple service disciplines (education services, field services, professional services, support services), which track both practices and results. Practices are business processes; results are metrics. The intent is to identify specific nonstandard processes that may be hindering your metrics performance, or to link above-average metrics with best-practice processes. Start with metrics that are below industry average and identify the related practices for review.

« Key Lessons Learned from Chapter 6 »

Customer service is a very technology-heavy operation, and most companies have multiple technology projects in various stages of implementation at any given time. With the large budgets required to purchase and implement a new tool, companies must do everything they can to ensure project success. Key lessons learned from this chapter include:

- **Process over technology.** Although companies that have had a technology project fail almost immediately begin blaming the vendor, in my experience, the most common reasons for project failure have less to do with the technology itself and more to do with the company's business processes. The truth is, you can have project success with most tools on the market. But if your groups can't communicate, if the data you capture isn't consistent across geographies, if escalation guidelines are constantly morphing, no product on the market can overcome your process problems.

- **Eliminate "changephobes" from the project team.** New technology projects are a great opportunity to refine, streamline, and update processes. If someone on the project team seems resistant to change (the usual indicator is when you hear the phrase, "But we've always done it that way!"), consider replacing that individual on the project team. He or she will bog you down at every turn.

- **Get third-party process input.** I have done projects with many companies that had process problems they couldn't figure out after months or years of study, but as an outsider, the core problems were obvious to me immediately. While each company has some unique characteristics, support processes are rarely radically different within a single industry (telco, financial services, high-tech, government, etc.), and an outside process expert will be able to shortcut identifying process issues and how to solve them.

TALES FROM THE VAULT:
OUT-OF-BOX FUNCTIONALITY

The very first conference I attended as an analyst was Oracle OpenWorld, held in New Orleans in February 2001, a few weeks after I started covering CRM and service desk software for Giga Information Group (acquired in 2002 by Forrester Research). I remember the conference for a couple of reasons.

President Bill Clinton had just left the White House after his 8-year term, and his opening keynote at Oracle OpenWorld was his first speech as a private citizen. I had never had the opportunity to hear a president speak live before, and Clinton really brought down the house. Unlike some other presidents, for whom English always seemed to be a second language, Clinton had this huge crowd in the palm of his hand. Regardless of political persuasion, his message about the importance of technology to improve and equalize global economies—and human rights—was very well received and inspiring.

The other high point of the conference for me was Oracle CEO Larry Ellison's keynote. I had an opportunity to meet Larry and hear him speak a few times prior, and he was definitely firing on all cylinders in New Orleans. I remember distinctly when he said, "Oracle software meets your business processes 80 percent out of the box. For the other 20 percent, you should consider changing your processes to match our out-of-box approach." Now, I'm sure it was worded slightly differently, but that was the gist of what he said. And the audience booed.

For the last decade, I've revisited what Larry said a million times in my head. And you know what? I think he was right. Oracle (and SAP, and NetSuite, and Microsoft, and FrontRange, and all the other CRM vendors) spends a tremendous amount of effort working closely with customers in each vertical market to understand best-practice processes, and they included those in the product. Keep in mind these software vendors "eat their own dog food," especially Oracle, meaning they use their own technology internally, warts and all. If the biggest software firms in the world use these packaged processes—and seem to do so with great success—then why are you arguing about keeping your old way of doing things?

I worked for a CRM vendor, and I've seen companies take beautifully designed process flows and rip them out, not even evaluating why the process was designed the way it was, and replace it with their own processes that had never worked well. I've seen companies insist on adding their own workflow objects (ensuring they will never be able to upgrade the system again without considerable work) that replicated existing technology because they were so convinced they were unique that they refused to use the identical out-of-box functionality.

If you are implementing any technology and find that the packaged processes are radically different from your own, I urge you to evaluate the packaged processes, look at how other companies handle the same process, and unless your existing process is clearly delivering accelerated revenue or lower costs, please consider adopting the industry best practice.

And if anyone on the project team says, "But, we've always done it that way!" fire him immediately.

Section 3

The Analyst Years

I REMEMBER TAKING A CAREER APTITUDE TEST IN HIGH SCHOOL, only to be told my ideal career choice would be working as a forest ranger. Not because of any profound love of nature—even at that age my idea of camping was a Marriott, not a tent—but because I had violent reactions to highly collaborative teamwork. As overly bright and overly ambitious people learn all too soon, when assigned to a team project, others usually leave the work to the overachiever. By college, I was already sick of doing 90 percent of team projects and never getting credit, or even acknowledgement, of my contribution.

No, forest ranger wasn't exactly right. But what the test did recognize was that I excelled at independent work. Give me problems to solve and I solved them quickly, efficiently, and sometimes using unconventional means. I was low-maintenance; I learned very quickly, took pride in having all the answers, and I preferred to be left alone to work. But this was in the very rural Ozark Mountains in the 1980s, and forest ranger was all they had to offer.

It turns out that industry analyst is Silicon Valley's version of forest ranger. You independently roam a segment of the technology industry looking for problems to solve, processes to automate, tools to make things easier. You identify ways that global forces impact your little slice of the world, and you have insights into how the success of your industry will impact the global economy. People look to you to have all the answers, and you never tire of learning new information.

Of course, now that I work from home, deep in the red-woods of the Santa Cruz Mountains, it could be that just a little bit of forest ranger has come true as well. Just don't ask me to go camping.

7 | Working with Industry Analysts

I'M SURE MANY PEOPLE HAVE NO IDEA WHAT AN INDUSTRY ANALYST does. I've been one for over a decade, and my family still has no idea what I do for a living. So here is the job description, in a nutshell: Industry analysts give advice.

Each analyst is an expert (or supposedly an expert, I'm sorry to say) on a set of business processes and technologies. There are analysts for supply chain, human resources, all areas of IT technology and infrastructure, as well as analysts who are experts on markets, such as telecommunications or financial services regulations. If you can name an industry, there is an analyst somewhere covering it.

The majority of analysts work for large analyst firms. There used to be dozens of firms, with lots of competing analysts, all with different opinions. Unfortunately, there has been tremendous consolidation among analyst firms over the last decade, and currently two firms, Forrester and Gartner, are the remaining giants. With fewer voices though, there is much less vision and leadership coming from the analyst ranks these days.

When I began as an analyst with Giga Information Group in 2001, Giga's analysts had an average of 15 years of experience in the industries they covered. Many of us had held marketing and development roles for software and hardware vendors, while others had been CIOs of large corporations. This approach to building an analyst firm is known as "star analysts," i.e., analysts who are recognized experts in their industry, sought after for media interviews and press quotes. Companies greatly appreciate advice from star analysts, as they have faced similar challenges many times and can provide real-world examples to accompany their advice.

Unfortunately, star analysts are expensive to employ. As the big firms have bought up the smaller firms, a new analyst model has emerged, which I call "ego-analysts." Today, analysts are hired out of college with zero experience, given a market to cover, and told to figure it out. Has the level of discourse suffered? Absolutely. Do companies receive questionable advice from analysts with no experience to draw upon? Absolutely.

I arrived at the term ego-analysts after my boss, an industry superstar who was (and still is) highly sought after by CEOs for vision and direction, was asked to speak to a group of new analysts fresh out of college. She was expecting questions about how to be a better analyst, what her research process was, how to make the tough calls. Instead, she only received one question, over and over, from every 20-something analyst in attendance: "How do I become famous like you?" No one wanted to do the hard work to become a recognized industry expert. They just wanted to be stars. They were ruled by ego, not intellect.

The large analyst firms don't care that IT buyers don't want technology advice from ego-analysts, because the majority of analyst-firm revenue now comes from technology vendors, not companies seeking technology advice. Vendors love inexperienced analysts because they will believe anything they are told and will parrot back vendor positions as opinions.

I remember meeting one of the new social media analysts from a big-name firm, who said he had just been briefed by an online community vendor I know well. When I asked what he thought of the product, he quoted the CEO's word-for-word description of why it was a good company, with zero value-add of his own. And that vendor—and other vendors whose messages he repeats verbatim to the press—absolutely loves this analyst, and uses him constantly for press quotes and webcasts because he'll say what they want.

Large vendors pay $10,000 a day plus expenses for analysts to come spend a day at corporate headquarters, being briefed on the latest products and features, hoping the analyst will write about the product positively and recommend them to technology buyers. And it works. When the only information an analyst learns is through these paid briefings, their view of the market becomes out of touch with reality over time.

Though influencing industry analysts is certainly easier today for vendors than it was in the past, it doesn't mean analysts are always quick to support a new vendor product or direction. I receive questions from vendors all the time about how to overcome a clear bias a Forrester or Gartner analyst has, or how to get visibility with key analysts when you can't afford the $10,000 a day to pay them to listen.

I'm writing this chapter for vendors, to give you some tips on how to work effectively with analysts. (And good luck navigating the egos.)

Getting the Briefing

A briefing is typically a 1-hour meeting in which a vendor provides information to an analyst about their products. First-time briefings focus more on company history, positioning, and product features. Follow-on briefings focus more on the latest release or major news such as acquisitions, mergers, or executive changes. Officially, briefings are free (not counting the full-day, $10,000 consulting briefings described earlier) and open to anyone. In reality, getting a briefing with an analyst is not that easy because:

- **You have to find an analyst covering your industry or technology.** Boy, I've had some huge arguments with vendors about this, usually because they want me to be interested in something I'm not. Analysts have published research agendas so you know what topics they are working on, and you need to pitch the briefing in terms that will interest the analyst. Just because you want to brief a specific high-profile analyst, that analyst may have no interest in your product because he will never write about it or answer inquiries about it. The briefing would not help him in his job, and it would not gain you any visibility.

- **Analysts only spend about 20 percent of their time doing briefings.** I surveyed coworkers while at Forrester to arrive at the 20 percent number, and I think it is fairly defensible. Writing research, performing advisory projects, and answering inquiries take up the majority of analyst time. Since doing briefings doesn't provide any revenue or help meet productivity goals (the number of briefings is not included in any analyst performance review that I'm aware of), some analysts only do one or two briefings a week, and getting on their schedule can be tricky.

- **Vendors that have big contracts with the analyst firm receive priority.** This is an ugly truth of the analyst world—the more you pay, the more analyst access you receive. Your largest vendors monopolize your time and pay dearly for the privilege. While analysts do accept briefings with unheard-of vendors because the briefing request included intriguing or innovative information, the fact is, there are few openings in the calendar for briefings with nonclient vendors, and even getting a busy analyst to read your request for a briefing may not happen.

So how do you request a briefing in such a way as to pique the interest of the analyst and improve the likelihood that he'll accept your request? My advice is to look at things from the analyst's point of view, and include information in your briefing request that will appeal to the analyst.

- **Analysts like to be first.** Being the first analyst to spot a trend and write about it is a great way to gain credibility and respect in the industry. In the briefing request, say that the adoption of certain products or features indicates a major new trend that you would like to discuss with the analyst. Since analysts are always on the lookout for their next research project, teasing them with a hot trend could definitely get their attention.

- **Analysts like to have all the answers.** Analysts spend a lot of time helping companies narrow their list of vendors for an upcoming technology project, and a lot of this process is about aligning unique product capabilities with the company's specific business problems. While every vendor says they are way ahead of their competition, it is rare for a vendor to have any real proof of this. If you truly have a competitive advantage—whether unique functionality in the product or innovative services that ensure project success and ROI—make sure your uniqueness is clearly visible in the briefing request.

- **Analysts like lots of visibility.** Some analyst firms reward analysts for the number of quotes and press mentions they receive, so visibility is always front of mind for the analyst. For the new breed of ego-analyst, visibility is the primary motivator. One way to almost guarantee an analyst will take your briefing is to say that it is a preannouncement briefing under nondisclosure, and that if the analyst takes the briefing, you will provide his contact information to the media as a knowledgeable expert when the announcement drops. This definitely works for mergers and acquisitions or significant leadership changes, but also for major product releases. Just don't tease an analyst with a hot preannouncement and then give them a not-so-hot briefing on a minor point release. You may never have that analyst's attention again.

Conducting the Meeting

Over the last 10 years of being an analyst, I'd estimate that I've had nearly 2,000 vendor briefings. Frankly, not that many are memorable. A few definitely stick out. One vendor started the briefing with the demo instead of saving it for the end (and then usually running out of time), because they felt if I saw the product, everything else would make sense. They were right. One of Silicon Valley's most respected CEOs used to make a point of dropping in for a minute anytime I was at a briefing at their headquarters, and he always quoted something from my most recently published report. Yes, I know the analyst-relations person handed him that factoid as he walked in the door—I sincerely doubt that he had ever read one of my reports. But the effort to show respect for my opinion certainly stroked my ego, and I saw many analysts change or soften positions toward this CEO and vendor because they liked the star treatment so much.

Of course, every analyst is different, so the ideal briefing format for one analyst may not meet 100 percent of the needs of another. But there are definitely guidelines for what to include—and what *not* to include—in the briefing that should keep you on track and meet the needs of all but the most egomaniacal of analysts.

Discuss Content Needs Up Front

At the time the briefing is scheduled, a good analyst-relations person will ask me what I want to get out of the briefing, and I'll tell them. A lot depends on what research projects I may be working on currently or have planned later in the year. I usually want to focus on customer success stories and return on investment (ROI) examples. For new vendors, I want to hear their view of the competitive landscape and why they win over other vendors. I may want information on specific features—like how multilingual content is managed within the database—if that is something I've been receiving a lot of inquiries about recently.

Sometimes I'm interested in adoption of tools by a certain market (like consumer support vs. enterprise support) or industry (telecommunications or financial services vs. high-tech). If you don't discuss this at the time the briefing is scheduled, be sure to ask the analyst at the start of the meeting if they have any specific things they want to discuss or focus on.

Don't Give Unwanted History Lessons

Boy, this is a major pet peeve of mine. Having now spent 25 years in the service and support industry, it drives me absolutely crazy when a vendor lectures me about industry history during a briefing, usually with a time line showing new channels being introduced, or the rise of social media, or evolving best practices. This is like waving a red flag in front of a bull, the implication being that you know more about the industry than I do, and you have to educate me before I can understand your product positioning.

When a vendor starts with a history lesson, I try to get them to move on by acknowledging I lived though their time line and understand their point. Sometimes that doesn't work; I assume the marketing person has memorized the slide deck and doesn't want to stray from the script. If you force me to sit through a history lesson, you can be sure I will start shooting holes in your time line, pointing out missing events, as well as providing colorful commentary, complete with insider information about the events they do have listed. Yes, I should be more patient. But unless I am picking up coverage on a brand-new market and have specifically asked for background, give me a little credit and skip the history lesson.

Proof Trumps Marketing-Speak

As my favorite Giga/Forrester boss, Erin Kinikin, used to say, "Analysts are from Missouri," playing on Missouri's reputation as the "show me" state. Analysts want examples of everything, and if you think we sometimes push too hard for customer examples or other proof points, it is because we've been lied to so many times.

My favorite example was when a large European software vendor was trying to prove that they were picking up new CRM customers and taking market share away from Oracle, whose acquisitions of CRM tools from Siebel, JD Edwards, and PeopleSoft gave them a huge majority share in the early 2000s. Responding to analyst pressure, the vendor printed an actual book listing every CRM customer, what modules they were using, and what they were using them for within the business. I attended one of the vendor's analyst events, and they held up this book in every meeting as proof.

There was only one problem: We weren't allowed to see the book. I was told if I wanted to see the book, I had to fly (at my own expense) to the vendor's corporate headquarters in Europe, and there was a room with a copy of the book that I could see—but not take out of the room.

Now, it could be that the book actually contained customer examples. Personally, I think the pages were blank, or they slapped a cover on a phone book. I am from Missouri, after all, and you have to show me. So, if you can't show me, and you come up with ridiculous reasons why you can't show me, you have now convinced me you are lying.

When you are creating the slides for your next analyst briefing, think about what proof you have for every marketing claim on every slide. If you don't have proof, skip the marketing-speak. In fact, how about only covering customer case studies, illustrating how companies are solving multiple complex business problems with your solutions? If you explain your competitive advantage using real-world customer examples, I will believe you and will be more likely to help promote your story.

Invest in Graphics

There are people who are incredibly graphically oriented. J.B. Wood, TSIA's CEO, is one of those people. He has a knack for taking an incredibly complex idea and creating a graphic that perfectly illustrates everything in a single image that would take five pages of writing for me to explain. This is not a talent I possess, I'm sorry to say. If this is not a talent you possess, please hire someone to do the graphics for you.

When you are trying to build support for a new idea, a new product, a new market segment, whatever, having a brilliant graphic can do much of the work for you. As an example, the early diagrams for CRM that showed customers at the center of the sales/marketing/support suite changed the way people thought about CRM. For niche vendors, having a graphic that shows where their solution sits in the IT CRM/enterprise resource planning (ERP) ecosystem can create instant understanding from analysts and buyers.

But muddled, overcomplicated diagrams just confuse people. I've seen some unbelievably bad graphics, the most common sin being trying to illustrate product depth and breadth, but instead, showing only a mess of tiny boxes and a two-point font that you couldn't read with a magnifying glass. There are a few other graphics slides I hope I never have to see again in a briefing:

- **The requisite slide of customer brands.** The point of this slide is to show off all the big brands the vendor has as customers, so they cut and paste every customer's logo on a single slide. Once again, to an analyst, this is like waving a red flag at a bull. I pride myself on knowing what products major companies use, and when their logo shows up on your slide—and I know they are using your competitor's product—I will want to know why. Usually it is because the competitor has the primary implementation, and this vendor has some small departmental implementation buried within corporate. I never see one of those logo slides without asking for examples of how specific companies are using their tool. More than half the time, the person giving me the briefing has no information on that customer, further eroding my faith that the logo company is really using the vendor's product in any significant way.

- **A competing analyst's slide.** One of the easiest ways to alienate an analyst—especially an ego-analyst—is to quote glowing reviews from a competing analyst firm. I've seen Forrester analysts explode when a vendor presented a Gartner Magic Quadrant as proof of their domination of a market. I'm sure Gartner analysts feel the same when a vendor tries to prove a point by showing a Forrester Wave. Those are great slides to use with media and prospects, but don't shove another analyst's views in my face—I'll just try to prove them wrong.

- **Company history.** The first time I speak with a vendor, getting some background on the company is helpful. Personally, I tend to do quite a bit of research on a company before I speak to them the first time; I think going into the briefing with a good bit of background helps make the meeting more productive. On subsequent briefings, I no longer want to see that company history slide, and I resent spending precious briefing time rehashing your history, which I already know. Often the analyst knows more about the company's history than the marketing person giving the briefing.

The final thing I want to discuss about working effectively with industry analysts is knowing when to use them. The majority of vendors prefer to brief the analysts only when a new product is being launched. The problem with this is that if I identify a feature hole or bad user interface (UI) element, there's no time to change it in the product. In a perfect world, the analyst should be engaged at all points of the product life cycle.

- **Requirements gathering.** When preparing the original marketing requirements document (MRD), submit an inquiry to your top analysts asking them about emerging trends and what constitutes "bleeding edge" today. Not only will the analyst hopefully provide useful insight for the MRD, but you've also stroked the analyst's ego by asking for his help early in the cycle.

- **Wireframes.** I spent time during my vendor years doing UI design, and I continue to focus on the UI when I am briefed on new tools. Many vendors have requested a briefing or submitted an inquiry asking me to review the wireframes (UI mockups) for applications currently in development. Not only did this allow me to spot problems early so that they could be fixed before the product was released, but I was flattered to be asked for my input during the design phase.

- **Preview product announcements.** There are a number of vendors who send me drafts of press releases to review before they announce new products or services or major company events. I've often added a section to highlight a critical competitive differentiator the vendor overlooked or gave them verbiage to use that strengthened the overall press release. This also feeds into analysts being prebriefed on major announcements — we love feeling like we are on the "inside."

- **Product launch.** When the product actually launches, this is when the analyst usually gets briefed on the release for the first time. And if the analyst hasn't had any visibility into the requirements phase, the wireframe phase, or the product announcement, he will try very hard to find fault, and it is usually phrased like this: "You can't release the product with that ridiculous UI. Why in God's name did you not ask me for input 6 months ago?" If you've involved the analyst all along the way, he will likely be your advocate and offer to field media calls about the launch.

The bottom line: Involve the analyst early and he becomes vested in your success. Blindside the analyst with a new release and he will continue looking until he finds fault.

« Key Lessons Learned from Chapter 7 »

This chapter was intended for technology vendors who depend on analyst coverage to raise visibility and influence buying decisions. However, now that service organizations are assuming higher profiles within product companies, services marketing should definitely target briefing key analysts annually on customer success. Here are some key lessons learned regarding working with analysts:

- **Analysts are not paid to do briefings.** Outside of paid advisory time, analysts do not receive any credit or recognition for the number of briefings they attend. As analysts are pushed to do more consulting and less writing, they have even less time for vendor briefings. You have to pitch the briefing request to the analyst with a message targeted specifically to that analyst's coverage area, pet topics, and stated research agenda or you have little chance of capturing his interest. If all else fails, offer him a prebriefing on your next big announcement under nondisclosure agreement—that usually piques analyst interest.

- **Make the briefing interactive.** Analysts hate to be marketed to. While all vendors create an official launch deck, when holding a briefing with a crucial analyst, don't be afraid to stray from the planned agenda to hit the areas of most interest to him. And definitely leave time for discussion. Personally, I like to have a discussion with a vendor, not a presentation from them. If you don't give me a chance to give feedback all along the way, you may miss out on insights like, "Your competitor just launched an identical campaign," or "I've had a dozen calls about this over the last month, and the term used is 'X,' and you are calling it 'Y.' "

- **Involve the analyst at every point in the product life cycle.** For analysts with high visibility or influence for your market, don't wait until the project launch to brief the analyst. Log an inquiry about product requirements, naming conventions, functional competitiveness, UI design, or launch messaging, keeping them in the loop all throughout the development and launch process. They are much more likely to be on your side than if you only update them once the product is out the door.

TALES FROM THE VAULT: PET PEEVES

I was involved with several programs at Forrester to coach vendors on effective analyst relations. At some point I surveyed analysts and vendors to find out what their pet peeves about each other were, and the list made for interesting reading. I've recently leveraged social media channels to gather feedback to update those lists, and here they are for your amusement:

Top Five Vendor Pet Peeves about Analysts

1. **Analysts that think they know everything about your business.** Condescension is never appropriate, but it is, unfortunately, all too common. Especially galling is a new analyst who starts lecturing a vendor on product strategy during the very first briefing.

2. **No review or insufficient time for review of research material.** Analysts publish on tight schedules, especially when a report is about a big announcement and the analyst wants to be "out in front" of the news. But giving vendors less than 48 hours to review anything is unrealistic, especially if it is a longer report that needs to be reviewed by multiple parties within the vendor. If a fast turnaround is required, a good analyst lets the vendor know the report is coming so they are ready to review it and provide feedback within the time window. Analysts should never blindside a vendor with a surprise report and expect an immediate turnaround, but from what I hear, this happens all too frequently.

3. **Analysts that aren't engaged . . . especially during briefings.** In the old days, analysts took notes on paper, and there was less worry of losing their attention. But now that

analysts sit perched behind laptops, typing through briefings, you sometimes wonder what they are typing about. I've heard horror stories of vendors who paid analysts to come to an advisory session, and the analysts spent the entire meeting checking e-mail and shopping on Amazon. If this happens to you, call your account rep and complain loudly. If the research firm offers a money-back guarantee (Forrester does), ask for a refund.

4. **Painting a vision that is unachievable . . . for vendors and for customers.** I know I am guilty of this sometimes. Analysts spend all of their time in ivory towers, where every trend is predictable, every problem has a solution, and everything would be better if only they were in charge. In many ways, we live in a fantasy world of how things should be. We are also *way* ahead of the curve, looking at the bleeding edge and sometimes forgetting that the real world may be 18 months to 2 years behind that bleeding edge. If the analyst is too far out there, line them up to talk to some customers who can bring them back down to real-world business problems.

5. **The age-old concern: pay-for-play.** Because you don't pay the amount of retainer/services that Fortune 100 companies do, you get less service (or inclusion in reports), but you are told you don't. Pay-for-play is real, and it happens in two major ways. The first is by dominating the analyst's time so he recommends you because you are all he knows. When I became an analyst in 2001, I was writing 30 to 40 research reports a year. I was encouraged to do consulting, but it wasn't a requirement. When I left Forrester, analysts were only required to write approximately seven reports a year, but they were required to do extremely high amounts of consulting . . . or else. Today's analysts primarily spend time with vendors who pay them, and, of course, when the analyst is asked for a customer example, the first thing that comes to mind will

be the paying vendor's examples. By dominating an analyst's time, they end up dominating the analyst's research.

The second way pay-for-play comes into effect is more blatant. I've heard horror stories of vendors saying, "I pay you X dollars a year, and I'm canceling my contract today if you don't improve my ranking in your research report." Unfortunately, sometimes that works. I once was publishing a CRM market overview, and one of the big vendors was furious that I didn't rate them first in every category. I was shocked, because frankly, I thought I was overly fair to them already and had given them high marks. When I refused to change my opinion, they threatened to "discredit my reputation in the marketplace." I'm still not sure what that meant, but being threatened with career destruction by a vendor who didn't like my fact-based opinion certainly pushed my buttons. I told them I wasn't changing anything, and then they called my boss, who agreed with my assessment and told the vendor to back off.

But that doesn't always happen, and today, with the lion's share of analyst revenue coming from vendors, the manager is more likely to ask the analyst to compromise to be sure they don't lose the account revenue.

Turnabout is fair play, so now I'll give analysts a chance.

Top Five Analyst Pet Peeves about Vendors

1. **Sending a 60-slide deck for a 30-minute call.** I've already talked about how many briefings analysts do and that we aren't paid to do them (except for consulting). Don't make the matter worse by sending me homework. I've received Power-Point decks with over 100 slides, multiple attached PDF case studies, press releases from the last five product launches, as well as multiple media clippings, all supposedly to "help me prepare" for a briefing. I'm sure it's fascinating reading, but I

simply don't have the time. Keep the content to what you can realistically cover in the time scheduled.

2. **Claiming the vendor is the "first" to do something . . . and then trying to justify it on the basis of a questionable metric.** I've seen vendors claim to be the first with a cloud solution in their market, the first to break one million page views per day, or the first to have referenceable customers, and when you push them on the facts, they always have some weird qualifier. "Well, we were the first product with a Spanish-language offering to do it," or "Well, we were the first company to do it with a female CEO." In other words, they are reaching into fantasyland to try to justify a claim that didn't impress me in the first place. Being the first to do something isn't that big of a deal; delivering positive results over and over again, in many different circumstances, is what makes analysts recommend you.

3. **"We'll be in your town, and we'd like to come by your office for a briefing."** Both Forrester and Gartner have company headquarters in the Boston area, and vendors seem to assume all analysts are located there. We are not. Analysts often work from home or satellite offices. I receive e-mails all the time asking if I'm available for lunch because a vendor is in San Diego that day and has some free time. TSIA may be headquartered in San Diego, but I live at the other end of the state.

4. **Spending the first 20 minutes on "positioning" and "messaging," and ignoring pleas to skip ahead.** As I discussed in the section on effective briefings, don't spend too much time on industry or company history; we want to hear what's new. I remember going with a group of analysts to a vendor's offices for an on-site briefing, and one executive spent nearly 30 minutes lecturing us on industry history despite multiple requests from us to move ahead. Finally, one analyst said,

"If you don't skip past the history lesson, I'm coming up there and moving the slides for you."

5. **Showing slides that contain glowing complimentary quotes or market sizing from a rival analyst firm.** Analysts love to prove their competitors wrong, and if it appears that a competing analyst firm is writing glowing things about you, I might just start looking for the other side of the story to prove them wrong. I'd like to think I am more mature than that, and personally, if you finished well in a Gartner Magic Quadrant or Forrester Wave, I'd consider that a valid proof point. But many analysts react loud and fast when a slide comes up with a rival firm's name, and I've seen analysts completely derail the meeting by picking apart their competitor's analysis for the remaining briefing time. Leave the analyst opinions out of your slides and avoid this situation entirely.

8 | Advice to Start-Ups

IN SILICON VALLEY, START-UPS ARE PRE-IPO TECHNOLOGY FIRMS—smaller firms building innovative products that they hope will sell like hotcakes and turn the start-up into the next Google or Apple. Of course, for every Google, there are a thousand companies that never make it to initial public offering (IPO). Sometimes the product isn't strong enough, but very often the failure is more about execution and management than technology.

I've worked for three start-ups, and I've spent time with hundreds—if not thousands—of start-ups over the last decade as an analyst. Though the products at each firm may be radically different, when viewed from a higher level, start-ups tend to have a lot in common, especially when it comes to evolving and maturing away from how things worked when the company had less than 100 employees. Those growth pains will make or break the company.

In this chapter, I've compiled 10 common challenges for start-up companies, in the hope that if you are a start-up or are considering seeking investment to launch a start-up, I can help you avoid the common causes for start-up demise.

1. **When it goes from "idea" to "company," you are no longer a democracy.** In the early days of a start-up, company founders tend to make group decisions. As key hires are added,

the growing number of employees are all asked to weigh in on product features, ad campaigns, brands and logos, partner strategy, and so forth. Every minute decision is broadcast to the whole company. While this attempt at maintaining a democracy may work when you have only 20 people, as your ranks grow, this approach becomes untenable. And when you grow beyond 100 and still try to reach consensus on every decision, your decisions will take weeks . . . then months . . . to make, and even small issues can turn into major company disagreements.

It is critically important that early on in the life of the company you establish department ownership and goals, agree on decision processes, and acknowledge that not everyone gets a vote in every decision. Strong companies have a rational balance of power between marketing, development, sales, and service, so groups can provide input on decisions that impact them, but the final decision must rest with one department or executive.

As an analyst, I know a start-up is in trouble when I go in for a briefing and the meeting is attended by dozens of people representing every department in the company. My questions are answered by multiple people at once—with conflicting answers—and my criticisms are often met with animosity and hubris. Analyst relations (AR) is a specialized field, and even if you don't have a dedicated AR person because you are still a small company, you must realize that not everyone should be involved in briefing analysts. When we hear lots of voices and conflicting information, we interpret that the company is in chaos. And I would never recommend a company in chaos.

2. **Defining, communicating, and building company values and culture.** In Silicon Valley, there is a lot of talk about high-tech company culture. Google, of course, is famous for its "Don't Be Evil" pledge, as well as free gourmet meals, bicycles for

getting around campus, and other employee perks the rest of us haven't seen since the start-up frenzy of the 1990s. They may work 80 hours a week, but in general, people who work for Google love the company.

I was not always so convinced that company culture made that big of a difference. Of course, now I realize that this is because I previously had worked for companies with a nurturing employee culture and assumed companies always operated that way. A huge eye-opening experience came when I worked for a start-up that shut down the company's e-mail system one weekend, printed out every employee's e-mail, and went through them one by one. On Monday, they fired every employee who had criticized a manager in an e mail.

Boy, oh boy, where do I even start? The situation seemed like a plot line out of *Dilbert™*. Clearly, there were some grumpy employees who weren't getting along with management, but this certainly isn't the way to address attitude problems. The remaining employees were so paranoid after that weekend that no one would ever speak their mind or provide constructive criticism again—we were too afraid we'd be fired. I left the company not long after that.

Today I realize that every company has a specific culture. Some are extremely casual, some are very slick and appearance-oriented, while others have a real backbiting competitive culture. One large tech company used to hire multiple people for the same job and tell the candidates that all but one of them would be fired after 3 months. They may be a high-performing company, but employees learn early on that they can't trust anyone.

My advice is to put a lot of thought into what the ideal culture for your company should be and what values and attitudes are required by employees to instantiate and reinforce that culture. When screening applicants, "culture fit" should be a primary consideration. This means that you have to say no to some extremely qualified people, because longer term, building a supportive, dynamic culture is more important than plugging in talent who will push back and fight the culture every day.

3. **Defining and sticking to a vision for the company: Don't be a hammer looking for a nail.** A dear friend worked for a company that had a major identity crisis. The company changed names three times, each name more ridiculous than the previous one. They started as a tech support product, morphed into a community platform, and before the creditors finally shut down the company, they had started marketing themselves as software for pharmaceutical trials. They had a couple of pieces of cool functionality, but they were unable to find a valid use case for the technology.

   Without a vision for the company, the sales team acted like they were a hammer looking for a nail, which means they had one solution to sell, but no one really wanted it, so they made deal after deal, promising to morph the product to fit the needs of the customer—whatever those needs might be. One of those customers, it turned out, was TSIA, but luckily, before my time. The product never went live for TSIA, because essentially what we bought was so far away from what the company delivered that they could never deliver anything that met our needs.

   It seems the most obvious piece of advice to tell start-ups is that they need to solve a clear, identifiable business problem, and they need to solve it for multiple companies across industries to gain credibility. But I have been surprised over the years at the number of start-ups that have received funding for a cool bit of technology with little or no applicability in the real world. If the business problems your products or services resolve are not on the list of issues "keeping executives up at night," go back to the drawing board. Hoping a market will materialize to support a cool idea is no way to run a start-up in today's economy.

4. **The first product management hire: Process over domain expertise.** I've been the first product management hire, and that is one difficult job. In the early days, start-ups develop products very organically, usually with a few geniuses building an application around a really great core idea or concept. There really isn't a process in the beginning—everyone just pitches in and gets the work done. But as the company starts to build a customer base and push for new sales, cool ideas sometimes need to take a backseat to market demands and customer commitments.

   This is the job for an experienced product manager. I've seen companies interview for up to a year, trying to find an expert on their niche market or infrastructure, while projects go off track and releases slip. The truth is, a good product manager doesn't have to know anything about your industry. Your first product manager hire is all about process, not technology.

   The first product manager must establish the template for marketing requirement documents (MRDs) or product requirement documents (PRDs), ensuring the document meets the needs of all involved. They need to establish the project flow, with leads and owners defined at each step. Oftentimes the biggest hurdle is not getting buy-in for the entire process—from MRD to development to quality assurance (QA) to beta testing to release—but getting people to stick to it. For the first year, you will repeatedly hear, "Oh, this is just a little project. We don't need to follow the big process." Yes, you do.

   Another key role of product management at technology start-ups is keeping everyone honest. One start-up I worked at had a bad habit of announcing new products 18 months out, when the product was nothing but a set of requirements.

They thought this was a great way to show that they were ahead of the competition, but when release dates kept slipping, ultimately they lost market visibility to the competing vendors who were actually delivering product, not just talking about it. This doesn't happen when product management is the authority on release dates and marketing announcements are built into the cycle.

5. **Product management must report to marketing, not development.** I'm sure there are examples of successful high-tech companies with product management reporting to engineering, but in my experience, it is a recipe for disaster. I've run product management for two companies, and have reported to both development and marketing. While I admit the stress level of the job may have been lower when I was part of development, the releases are more likely to be delivered on time and with higher-quality content when product management reports to marketing. Here's why.

   Just like the U.S. government has separate executive, judicial, and legislative branches to ensure that there is a balance of power, having marketing own product management ensures that development delivers what the market demands and what customers require—not what the developers want to build.

   When I worked in development, I would go through the same process of requirements, gathering and publishing an MRD or PRD that everyone (sales, marketing, development, professional services, QA, and support) all had to buy-off on. From there, the projects tended to go all to hell.

   Developers didn't like my approved designs, so they would come up with their own "cool" UI controls that may have looked good, but were inconsistent with the platform and ultimately created confusion for users. Frontline engineers would drop features they didn't want to build or come up with lazy solutions that didn't meet all the requirements. When

I complained, I was completely ignored, because I reported to the same vice president of development that the engineers did, and he always sided with his developers.

Marketing would end up with a release that was usually 6 to 9 months late, and missing key features that they had already announced to the industry. Sales would complain that the release delivered bore no resemblance to the release they approved. QA would complain about all the nonstandard processes and UI elements that added even more time to the release schedule, as they had to start all over with testing plans. And always, the product manager was to blame. We had zero influence or control, but total responsibility.

When product management reports to marketing, this doesn't happen. Oh, don't get me wrong, you will still have features dropped, shifts in UI, and endless project delays, but at least you have the authority to argue anytime someone strays from the approved marketing requirements. Sales is usually on marketing's side, and in my experience, so is the CEO. I've seen some unbelievably childish and egomaniacal development vice presidents in my time, but I've never seen one who could out-argue, out-negotiate, or out-scream the marketing vice president.

6. **Making the move from customer-driven to market-driven.** Every successful start-up reaches a point where many of the fun things that defined them as a start-up company need to change as they grow into a large, publicly traded firm. Lots of policies that worked when you had less than 100 people don't scale when the company is reaching 1,000 employees, such as bringing dogs to work, catered lunches, Friday beer busts, and ultracasual dress codes. But what I see as the biggest change start-ups need to make is a transition from being 100 percent customer-driven to becoming at least 50 percent market-driven.

A great way to tell if a company has made this shift is to attend their annual user conference. I remember attending a small company's user conference and being impressed by how folksy it was. Everyone was very casual, the small number of customers and employees all seemed to know each other, and everyone was relaxed and open to sharing ideas.

I went back to that same company's user group a few years later, after the company had grown dramatically and gone public. The event was big, the keynote sessions were packed, the audience was mostly dressed in business-casual, but there were also quite a few suits as well as a large contingent from some military customers wearing full dress uniforms. Clearly, the company had gone from start-up to a successful firm, but the company culture hadn't changed. At all.

When the CTO of the company came out to give his futures presentation, he was barefoot, wearing a tie-dyed shirt and torn jeans. With his long and unkempt hair, he looked more like a beach bum than an executive, and there were gasps from the audience. I was sitting behind some of the military contingent, and I kept hearing a single word over and over: *disrespect*.

There comes a time when companies need to grow up. Customers want to know that they invested in a professional company, and prospects want to know that they are selecting a mature organization. I don't care how big your smile is—the meeting with a group from a European financial services firm will not go well if your executives are barefoot and dressed in hippie garb.

7. **Don't keep executives around because you want to avoid paying the "firing bonus."** Let me be blunt: The executive team that took you from zero to 100 customers is *not* the same group of executives that will take you from 100 to 1,000 customers. It takes a very unique set of skills to evangelize and

create a brand-new market. You need visionaries. You need domain experts. You need out-of-the-box thinkers. You need customer zealots. But once that market is established, you need a whole other set of skills to make the company grow.

Marketing and sales are two departments for which this is especially critical. But many companies struggle to accept the fact that new blood is required, and I've heard multiple start-ups tell me that they know they need a new vice president of sales who understands multiple verticals and volume selling, or a new vice president of marketing with analyst relations and media experience, but they don't want to fire their existing vice presidents because of the "firing bonus" they would have to pay to get rid of them.

Bite the bullet and pay them off. They aren't walking away from this gravy train on their own, and you can never grow with them on board. Ultimately, those employees will thank you, because if their talent lies in building a market, they should find another start-up and repeat their success over and over again. Let someone with more experience in mature industries pick up the ball and run with it.

For companies that delay going public and seek multiple rounds of funding from venture capitalists, this decision will be made for you. Venture capitalists like executives with a history of growing businesses and will definitely make some changes to your vice president- and C-level team. If you want any say in the matter, take care of business yourself before the venture capitalist forces you to.

8. **Avoid "big fish in a small pond" syndrome when hiring.** When you decide to take the big jump and hire some new executives, recruit professionals with experience in your current market—not just the market you wish you were in. This is something I've seen happen over and over and over within the CRM world. Smaller firms with success selling to small and

medium-size companies—a huge market for CRM—decide to bring in executives who ran global CRM sales for SAP or Oracle or another huge global firm.

First of all, these folks don't know much, if anything, about the midmarket, and they are so enamored with $1 million–plus deals that they won't show respect for your smaller customers— the bread and butter of your company. Every time this happens, the vendor announces a major push into large enterprise deals. And just how much success do you think the small firm with nothing but small customers will have selling into huge enterprises? Oh, they'll close some deals because they will give away the product for next to free to get the business. But then they are stuck with these large companies as customers—and a product only suited for a much smaller firm.

About a year after one of these "big fish" hires, the executive leaves the company, the large team of enterprise sales folks they recruited are cut, and the company has to go back to pleasing the midmarket, who they spent the last year alienating and ignoring.

There is nothing wrong with having enterprise expansion plans. But hiring executives who can't serve your current market while you gear up to tackle the new market will fail every time.

9. **Walk away from customers you will never satisfy.** Start-ups are so desperate for deals that they tend to overpromise to close business. It is very hard for a tiny start-up to meet the needs of a huge global company, and as much as you want that big brand as a reference, you have to face facts: Unless you can meet their needs, they won't be a reference. And meeting their needs is pretty unlikely when they require more assistance than you have available to give.

I remember working for a start-up that was so desperate to close a deal with a huge global software vendor that we agreed to lots of product changes, crazy discounting, and free implementation assistance. In my recollection, this $70 billion customer was never referenceable for us. The implementation went on for at least 2 years, and a lot of that was spent building custom versions of out-of-box capabilities because of crazy things such as not liking our database table and field names.

When the company finally went live with our software, their implementation was about 90 percent custom. They could never upgrade because of all the custom tables and workflow objects they created. They would endlessly complain about missing features, most of which were added in subsequent releases, but they couldn't take advantage of the new code because they couldn't upgrade, leading to even more custom development.

I know that when you are a young company, having a huge brand on your customer list is a big deal. But you have to think long and hard about the pros and cons of having a huge global enterprise as a customer when you are still a struggling start-up firm. In most cases, the tail will end up wagging the dog.

10. **Business leaders don't care about your technology, so have a message for both IT and business buyers.** The main difference between being an analyst for Forrester and being an analyst for TSIA is that at Forrester, our members were CIOs, and at TSIA, they are business users, such as the vice president of customer service or the vice president of professional services. When you talk to IT about a pending technology purchase, they want to know about operating systems and databases, multithreaded application program interfaces (APIs), integration code, scalability, and ownership costs. When you talk to business users about a pending technology purchase, they focus on use cases, functionality, usability, employee adoption, and end-user training.

As a vendor, you need to have the "walk and talk" for both audiences, but I find that many start-ups are so enamored with their own technology that they can't articulate the business value or have a meaningful dialog with business users.

Before the rise of cloud computing, IT heavily influenced— if not outright owned—technology purchases. The single most common complaint from business users who hate their current CRM or incident management application is that IT picked the product and "shoved it down our throats," not allowing the business users any input. When cloud solutions became available, offering business users targeted controls for configuration and customization, many companies jumped at the chance to select their own technology without involving IT. In fact, many early on-demand buyers told me that keeping IT out of the project was their primary reason for going with a cloud solution.

So, for start-ups selling on-demand solutions, if you don't have the pitch down for business users, you are in big trouble. I wonder sometimes when I'm sitting through a briefing with a start-up, and their CTO starts talking Java versions, Perl, Python, Ruby, and PHP, who he thinks his audience is? If that is the briefing you give a vice president of service, I guarantee you won't get the business.

« Key Lessons Learned from Chapter 8 »

Advice to start-up technology firms may feel like an odd fit for a book focused on customer service, but in documenting 25 years' worth of lessons learned, I found I had amassed a great deal of best-practice advice for small technology firms trying to make the leap to a midsize or large firm. From working at several start-ups, to having briefings with start-ups every week for over a decade, to doing advisory projects with many start-ups during my time at Giga and Forrester, and now having spent 6 years giving advice to many small TSIA members, clearly there are many common problems among start-ups. Some key lessons learned from this chapter include:

- **Growing up is hard to do.** Much of my advice to start-ups relates to moving from being entirely customer-focused to being more market-focused. This is such a difficult time for companies, and it is the point at which many companies fail. The bottom line is that the leadership and processes that got you to 100 customers is probably not the leadership and processes that will get you to 1,000 customers. Companies that aren't willing to change are unlikely to make the transition beyond start-up firm.

- **Product management should report to marketing.** I know this is a controversial view, as some companies have product management within development, especially when the product is extremely technical. But in my experience, product management is only successful when they have the power to stand up and fight for requirements (especially when faced with lazy developers), and the vice president of marketing has the clout to do that. The vice president of development will side with his developers, overriding product management, every time.

- **The messaging shouldn't be too far out in front of the products.** Back in the late 1990s, vendors had a bad habit of announcing new platforms (the move from C++ to .COM) and new features (from phone-centric to multichannel) more than a year before the product released, and both customers and analysts stopped believing anything they said. I don't think the problem is as bad today as it was, but I still see companies making very aggressive announcements I know they don't have the resources to deliver to the market. Being too far out in front of the product only creates confusion in the market, and for a start-up company, one well-publicized missed product deadline may be difficult to recover from.

TALES FROM THE VAULT: FIRING CUSTOMERS

At my first start-up, one of our customers was horrible to deal with. Now, I had been a customer of this company long before I became an employee, so I knew this customer from user-group conferences and beta test panels. I knew they had a reputation for being demanding and hard to work with, but I had no idea to what degree.

Once I joined the company, this customer preferred to work primarily with me and another employee who also had been a customer, assuming we would be more responsive to their needs because we had an established relationship. But the customer was so abusive to us that it became quickly obvious that they couldn't be made happy—they were happy being miserable.

For over a year I made at least two visits a month to see this customer, trying to put out one fire or another. They were pushing the product to do things it wasn't designed to do, and they often took coding matters into their own hands, creating custom code that didn't work—then holding us responsible for it. Admittedly, they also had quite a few valid concerns, but they had no interest in going through the process of adding enhancements through the release cycle, always demanding whatever it was be fixed in the next patch or they would stop using the product.

The final straw was when this customer decided to stage a coup d'état at our annual user conference. In the middle of a general session, they stood up and started shouting, demanding their requested enhancements be delivered immediately, and shouting for other customers to stand up and join them. It was chaos. It was also so unbelievably unprofessional and galling that I refused to meet with them anymore, and luckily, my management supported me. I think they knew I had been pushed too far and abused too often to be empathetic.

I put together a spreadsheet showing how much this customer paid us annually and compared that with the amount of money we spent discussing their almost daily threats, flying development teams on-site to see them and be ridiculed in person, their refusal to do any reference calls or even include their logo in our list of customers, and their horrible behavior that hurt our image at conferences. Clearly, we were losing money on this account. I went to our CEO, armed with my spreadsheet, and suggested we fire the customer.

We didn't fire the customer, but after seeing the numbers in black and white, and finally realizing this group of controlling tyrants was never going to be a reference account for us (or anyone else, for that matter), at least we stopped bowing down to them and started saying no. It turns out that when we called their bluff, they didn't walk away after all.

9 | Future of Customer Service: Impact of Video

Early in my analyst days in 2001, remote-control software was just becoming popular for IT help-desk support. Help-desk agents could "take control" of an employee's desktop computer remotely to troubleshoot and resolve problems without the painful process of walking the customer through complex diagnostics. IT loved the tool, which cut incident-handling time and drove up first-contact resolution. But employees were initially nervous about a stranger accessing their computer.

I interviewed end users and found that while they were uncomfortable with the remote access, they liked the tool because their problems were solved faster and easier. At that time, I coined the phrase, "convenience overrides paranoia."

This phrase, which I have since started calling "Ragsdale's Law," has come in handy over the years. I used it again when remote-control software made its first appearance in external customer support, leveraged first by computer and application vendors, then by Internet service providers (ISPs). I used it again when remote monitoring became common in enterprise support for enterprise hardware and software deployments. And I used it again when customers—and technology companies—initially struggled with privacy aspects of social networking.

In this era of "sexting" scandals, large-scale credit card fraud, and never-ending phishing schemes, a healthy dose of paranoia is a good thing. But as history has shown us, and I'm sure the future will continue to illustrate, convenience wins every time.

I'm gearing up for the next application of Ragsdale's Law, and the time is almost here: video support interactions. Video is already changing many aspects of support, and I believe we are just seeing the tip of the iceberg. The impact of video is in three primary areas: knowledge management, education, and in the future, customer interactions via video. Video in knowledge management is already proving its value for early adopters. Video in education is in the early phases, with technology available but adoption coming at a slow pace. Video for support interactions is finding use cases in other industries, but is absolutely coming soon for technology support.

Increasing Knowledge Consumption with Rich Media

As technology grows more complex, customers ask more questions about how to use the products. One of the major North American mobile providers told me that they now receive an average of five calls for every customer that switches to a new smartphone, because each device now contains so many features—and little or no documentation—that consumers simply aren't able to figure out how to use the phone on their own. Enterprise hardware and software also grows more complex and sophisticated with each new release, and there are fewer IT resources available in most companies to help employees understand and navigate technology.

We typically think of technical support as spending their time researching unusual problems or trying to force a down system back online. But according to TSIA data, support engineers today are spending the majority of their time answering procedural questions, i.e., how to do something within the applications. The applications themselves are too complicated for end users to figure out on their own.

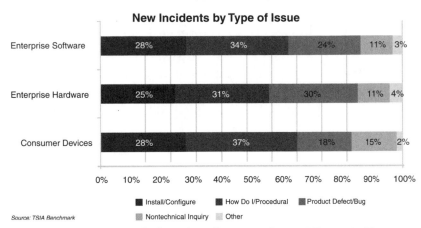

Figure 3.9.1: "How Do I?" Questions Represent Largest Percent of Issues

As seen in *Figure 3.9.1*, a total of 37 percent of consumer incidents, 31 percent of enterprise hardware incidents, and 34 percent of enterprise software incidents are from customers needing help using product functionality. Installation/configuration questions and reports of product bugs or defects come in second or third in all three industries.

Theoretically, procedural issues should be the easiest for customers to solve using product documentation and self-service. However, less documentation is provided with today's technology. In lieu of a user guide, many consumer devices are shipped with bare-bones documentation that includes a URL where online help can be accessed. Enterprise high-tech firms have made massive cuts to technical documentation teams, and printed reference manuals are rarely provided.

As application processes become more intricate and complex, clearly written instructions are more difficult for knowledge authors to create, and even more difficult for many customers to follow. Customers complain when written procedures are provided if the procedures gloss over important details or make mistaken assumptions about the skill level of the reader, thus preventing customers who find the correct help file or knowledgebase article from successfully absorbing the content and following its advice.

How, then, can companies take their existing knowledgebase content and make it more easily consumable by customers of all skill levels? Rewriting all of the content, migrating to new knowledgebase technology, or adding additional enterprise search tools are all options, but the cost of each of these approaches may be prohibitive and might not solve the complexity issue. For many TSIA member companies, the answer is to add rich media to their existing knowledgebase articles, either as embedded elements or attachments, which illustrate how to execute a process or a recovery procedure in such a way that even the most novice of customers can easily and successfully follow along.

And the cost to create these videos is not prohibitive, with most companies using an existing screen-capture tool to record videos showing how to navigate an application to complete a procedure or task. Customers love the video approach, which allows them to follow along step-by-step, starting and stopping the

Figure 3.9.2: HP Support Channel on YouTube

video as many times as necessary to follow the procedures and complete the task.

A great example of leveraging video to increase self-service would be HP Consumer's dedicated HP Support Channel on YouTube, as seen in *Figure 3.9.2*, with libraries of how-to videos, tutorials, troubleshooting tips, technology overviews, and general product information.

On-Demand Video: The End of Classroom Training

In the consumer world, the line between video content for customer support and video content for customer training is very gray. Consumer devices do not have a history of paid training classes (Apple's Genius Bar subscriptions being a rare example), with the only training available historically being the product user manual. As products grow more complex and user manuals are replaced by "quick start" guides—or eliminated entirely—videos have proven an effective way of showing customers how to use device features or navigate configuration controls.

Things are quite different in the B2B, or enterprise support, world. Enterprise hardware and software firms have a long history of monetizing training classes. While basic or limited training may be included with the purchase of new technology, this is usually limited to one seat in the next upcoming system administrator class. To train additional power users or administrators, and to learn additional information such as customizations, integrations, and how to perform major upgrades, companies pay the vendor for additional training classes, often conducted at the vendor's headquarters over a period of 3 to 5 days. These are traditional instructor-led, classroom-style classes, with a price tag of around $4,000, plus airfare, hotel, and expenses.

The traditional classroom approach will slowly be replaced by video training for multiple reasons, including:

- **The time commitment is unrealistic.** With multiple back-to-back economic downturns over the last decade and the rise of on-demand tools reducing IT's workload, IT organizations in North America have been shrinking, with each IT administrator doing double or triple duty on multiple systems. Expecting these workers to disappear for a week at a time for training is unrealistic—they are simply too overworked and valuable to be gone for extended periods. Video training allows IT administrators to schedule chunks of training into their day, while remaining available for regular duties as well as requests and problems that may arise.

- **Classroom training is less effective for some demographics.** It could be that Generation X, the group that followed the Baby Boomers, was the last age group that found traditional classroom training to be effective. For Generation Y, those in their 20s now entering the workforce, life has been a series of YouTube videos, chat and Instant Messenger, social networking, and movies on-demand. Younger employees learn differently, and at a different rate, and tend to find classroom training uninspiring, hard to relate to, and ultimately not very effective. Video training, however, fits into the Generation Y paradigm, offering a more engaging platform with collaboration features available as needed.

- **Classroom training is expensive to deliver.** I delivered classroom-style training to new system administrators for one of the vendors I worked for. In my experience, it wasn't a very profitable venture. Yes, we did have a room full of paying attendees. But once you factored in my time (including travel and expenses since classes were usually not held in my hometown), rental fees for the facility and classroom, training manuals and additional content that had to be copied, and refreshments for attendees, we barely broke even on training classes. Video content is delivered once, and watched over and over for possibly years, maximizing profits by eliminating delivery and facility costs.

For the same reasons, video training is catching on for employees, not just customers. By streaming video tutorials to a support technician's desktop, you can maximize their time by filling lulls in inbound support traffic with short learning segments. Learning management systems can be used to track who has viewed which videos and completed which modules, including quizzes to test content consumption and comprehension. With the alternative being pulling employees "off phone" for training—impacting service levels and customer satisfaction—video training for employees makes even more sense.

My view of the future of technology education is that content is created and streamed by channel, and customers can subscribe to a channel by named user or by an enterprise license. You could have channels of video content for end users who use the applications; other channels for administrators who need to know about implementation, upgrade, and customization; and special channels for upgrade advice.

Learning management systems (LMS) and learning content development (LCD) applications are expanding to make this transition to video easier. From managing registrations online, including credit card payments or third-party billing, to the creation and distribution of video content, technology is evolving to meet these needs. However, I suspect that in the future, training videos will be much shorter and more informal than in the past.

I recently spoke with a large TSIA member who converted their entire classroom training operation to an on-demand video library. At first, their approach was to replicate the formality of classroom training in a high-quality video. What they found is that customers are more likely to sign up for smaller, bite-size chunks vs. 5 days' worth of content, and they appreciated a less formal delivery, including lower expectations for high-quality production values.

At one of TSIA's recent conferences, a partner was debuting a new learning management system. When I talked to them about how companies were using it, they echoed my view of where we are going: Customers are creating large libraries of short, casual, quickly produced videos, not worrying about delivering an entire 3-day class in a single module or having high production values. Customers particularly are responding to videos made by product engineers or other subject-matter experts, even if they tend to have a monotone voice or are not very polished speakers. Video training allows every customer to have an audience with an expert.

Customer Interactions via Video: Get Ready

While everyone thinks that video for knowledge management and education is a great idea, anytime I start talking about bringing video interactions into the customer support center I see panic in everyone's eyes. And yes, there are certainly a lot of concerns to think about, like naked customers on video and having to help customers on bad hair days. But ultimately, I think Ragsdale's Law will apply once again: With the convenience and heightened level of service clearly possible by leveraging video, both customers and support management will soon get over the paranoia.

As seen in *Figure 3.9.3*, in the very early days of support, there weren't even dedicated support centers. Usually a single contact at the customer site had authorization to call an expert at

Evolution of Support Interactions

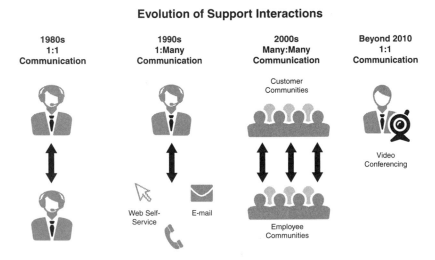

Figure 3.9.3: Evolution of Support Interactions

the vendor for support, possibly a developer or a quality assurance engineer. With no CRM, incident management, or knowledge-base tools, they would work one-on-one with the customer to solve the problem.

As technology expanded into every corner of corporations and homes, consumer call centers boomed and vendors established technical support centers for enterprise customers. By the 1990s, customers could even select an alternative to the telephone, such as e-mail, then the web, then chat, with ease of interaction being more important than who was helping you on the vendor side.

Over the last few years, the boom of online communities has again changed the customer-vendor dynamic, with customers helping customers and expert internal communities—including support, development, and product management—collaborating on customer problems and enhancement requests.

With new approaches to self-service and online communities helping answer less-technical questions, I believe the stage is set for the next evolution, taking us right back to where we started: a dedicated one-to-one relationship between customer and vendor, though this time around with the added intimacy of video conferencing.

Of course, interacting with customers via video isn't new; it just hasn't made it big in the technology industry. Financial services started using video with premier customers for financial planning and investment meetings post-9/11, allowing customers low-cost access to financial advice by eliminating the need for an expensive office in Manhattan for face-to-face meetings. Health care has been experimenting with video connections to allow doctors to check up on homebound patients, with devices to monitor vital signs remotely and video used for cursory examinations and well-being checks.

My prediction is that video will start in technical support with premier support services, such as having a technical account manager (TAM) dedicated to your account. In the past, TAMs made frequent site visits or were even located at the customer site to increase intimacy and build the relationship. Taking on a concierge role, a video TAM will recognize and greet each customer contact, personalizing every interaction. As a proof point, salesforce.com, the leading on-demand CRM vendor, offers video interactions to their premier customers today.

Obviously, some technology problems will be much easier to resolve using video. Think about troubleshooting and walking customers through procedures on a smartphone. How much easier would it be if you could see which buttons they were pushing, or if the support tech could demonstrate what you should do using the same model phone as the one you're using? How much more personal would the customer-vendor relationship be if the smiling face of the support tech was on your screen during a remote-control or web chat session? One TSIA member is putting cameras in customer equipment rooms so they can monitor how their customers use the equipment. These installations also give them the ability to coach their customers when repairs are needed. ("No, not that button; the big red button 2 inches to your right.")

Just like running into your neighbor at the grocery store or putting on a happy face for coworkers every day, once we get over the paranoia, answering the video phone will require no additional thought—other than making sure you aren't still wearing your pajamas when working from home.

How soon will we see wide adoption of video within customer support? Technology is already ready to go. One of the major suppliers of remote-control and desktop sharing tools tells me they already have video embedded in their platform for remote control and chat, but they just have it masked because its presence makes some companies uncomfortable. Clearly, we need some great examples and hopefully a positive ROI story to get things moving, but video is coming, whether we like it or not. My advice is to look for ways to use it before customers start demanding it and you lose control.

« Key Lessons Learned from Chapter 9 »

One piece of advice I received from many of my peers when writing this book was, "Don't talk about futures—it will all be obsolete too fast." As this book was memoir-focused, avoiding future predictions wasn't hard, but I couldn't resist including this final chapter on my current obsession—the impact video will have on service operations. Some key lessons learned from this chapter are:

- **Convenience overrides paranoia.** This phrase, which I call Ragsdale's Law, has been proven time and time again. Regardless of the change-management issues, customers will be fast to adopt any new channel or mechanism that allows them to solve their problems faster. Instead of coming up with all the reasons why video in service will be a problem, look for the use cases in which video can be successful. Like it or not, it is coming soon.

- **The largest percentage of customer issues is procedural.** When you ask support professionals about the type of customer issues they receive, they usually give complex technical problems as an example. But procedural or "How do I . . . ?" questions represent more than one-third of customer interactions. These are the questions most easily answered by self-service, and video walkthroughs of how to complete a process or task are definitely more consumable than long, written procedures.

- **High production values don't matter.** What I'm hearing from companies who have made the transition from classroom training to e-learning using video is that creating high-quality videos using a professional crew or studio is a waste of money. The generations that prefer just-in-time video training came of age with YouTube, and they consider simply produced videos featuring experts—not actors or paid presenters—to be far more valuable than professionally produced video content.

- **Video isn't just for customer interactions.** At a recent TSIA conference, I saw a vendor in the Expo Hall flying an unmanned camera-equipped drone around the room. A wireless headset and viewer allowed him to control the drone and zoom in with the camera. This was a great illustration of leveraging video for field service repair to get "up close and personal" with equipment, whether it is on top of a tower or on the side of an oil tanker. When evaluating how video can be used in service, look beyond customer interactions—the innovative ideas emerging are inspiring.

TALES FROM THE VAULT: PRAGUE

If you have managed to read this far, you know that I like telling stories. In fact, the genesis of this book was listing my favorite industry anecdotes and trying to fit them into a cohesive story line. There is one story, however, that I don't like to tell. Unfortunately, this one story seems to have taken on a life of its own, because a dozen times over the last few years I've had someone walk up to me at a conference or say at the end of a briefing, "I heard what happened to you in Prague."

From now on, anytime someone asks me about the Prague incident, I can just say, "You'll have to buy my book."

It was the summer of 2005, and I was heading to Europe to do some consulting work and speak at a conference—the absolute coolest part of an analyst's job. My first stop was Amsterdam, where I spent a day with a hot new knowledge management vendor talking strategy, and then had dinner with some of their customers, including the UWV, the Institution of Employee Insurance, the Netherlands' version of the Social Security Administration.

It was a fascinating dinner, especially hearing the head of service from a government organization speak passionately about helping customers (not citizens, not constituents, *customers*). This was something I found often in Europe—government agencies passionate about improving the lives of the average public— whether it was the Netherlands paying unemployed workers to take vacations or London's Borough of Sutton providing free e-mail accounts for citizens and installing free e-mail kiosks throughout the borough so everyone had easy access to e-mail. I had never heard anything like this from any of the North American government groups I had talked to—ever.

The next day I flew to Prague to speak at a Forrester confer-ence. I arrived on a Saturday afternoon and the conference began on Monday morning, so I planned to spend the weekend sight-seeing with some coworkers. Most of my peers were arriving on Sunday, so I took a taxi from the hotel to the only place in Prague I'd heard of—Wenceslas Square—and wandered around on my own. I strolled through the winding stone streets, walked across the Charles Bridge, and waited for the top of the hour to see the famous astronomical clock's procession of the Twelve Apostles in the Old Town Hall Tower. I went for dinner at some eatery down a side street off Wenceslas Square.

After dinner, I stopped at an ATM for some cash and headed back to the Square to catch a cab back to the hotel. The sun had not quite set, and there were lots of people on the sidewalks. The last thing I remember is the sound of people running up behind me, being hit from behind, and seeing the pavement rising up to meet my face. Then everything went black.

I woke up 15 hours later in a Prague hospital. I was in shock and in a lot of pain, and very confused. The staff barely spoke English, and they didn't seem able or willing to answer any of my questions. I kept asking how I got there and who brought me, and from what I could understand, the police had found me lying in the street, unconscious after being mugged, and had brought me to the hospital for care.

I caught a cab back to the hotel, and since my wallet had been stolen, at this point, I started calling to cancel credit cards. If you have ever tried to do this from a foreign country, you know just how difficult it can be: Credit cards have toll-free numbers on the back of them that don't work internationally. I started with Bank of America, wanting to cancel my ATM card and, hopefully, get a rush replacement. When I finally reached a live agent, I told her I was in shock, had just been released from the hospital after a violent mugging, and needed to get a replacement ATM card and have some money wired to me as soon as possible. Do you know what she said?

"It looks like you are prequalified for a mortgage; would you like to hear details about our mortgage rates today?" I said no. "It appears that you don't have our additional security package on your account, which would really help when these problems arise. Would you like to sign up today?"

I was in agony in a strange hotel room, having lost 15 hours of my life, and this clueless support agent was trying to upsell me! I declined all the offers, probably uttering a few obscenities along the way. And when I was told it would take 4 to 6 weeks for me to receive a new ATM card and that they couldn't wire money to me internationally, I understandably said good-bye.

My next call was to American Express. They immediately transferred me to a special group that dealt with customers in crisis, and the woman was so empathetic and willing to help me that I finally started to relax. She asked for a list of all of my other cards, took care of canceling them and ordering replacements on my behalf, and arranged to have a replacement American Express card and $1,000 cash waiting for me at a bank near the hotel in less than 24 hours.

Now *that's* service. When I got home, I upgraded to a Platinum American Express card. This is the kind of company you want to keep doing business with.

I had missed meeting my teammates for a tour of Prague Castle, and I knew people were wondering where I was. I placed a call to the senior Forrester manager at the conference, Dan Mahoney, to let him know what happened. Dan was amazing, making sure I had medical supplies, loaning me cash, and escorting me to the bank to collect the American Express card and wire transfer.

Monday morning came, and despite everyone telling me I should skip the conference and fly home, I put on my suit and did my conference speech. My face was one big patch of road rash, and I was walking slowly and painfully from the deep bruising, but the show must go on.

What can we learn from this story, other than that regardless of your size, you need to be cautious when traveling alone, especially when withdrawing cash from an ATM? There is definitely a lesson to be learned about customer service: Be there when your customers really need you, and they will be loyal forever.

Bank of America is frequently in the press with customer issues, be it gouging us with more fees, shutting down branches, or making huge profits at the expense of customers. But before my trip to Prague, I had a good relationship with Bank of America, and I thought they were on my side. When I called from a foreign country, hurt and needing help, all they tried to do was upsell me. My interpretation of the Bank of America brand changed that day. They clearly were only in it for the profit.

Contrast that with American Express, who solved my problem immediately and took away the stress and fear of being stranded overseas. They have a team in support dedicated to helping customers in dangerous or frightening circumstances, and those team members are clearly trained in crisis management and expert service skills. My already-positive view of American Express also changed that day—for the better. I'm a rabidly loyal customer, because I truly know that they are there for me when I need them.

As support professionals, I challenge you to ask yourself if your frontline agents or techs are trained to handle a customer in crisis. Consider introducing a special procedure for navigating these situations, which certainly includes breaking from traditional call scripts, and offer extensions. Being a customer steward means being there in good times and bad times and handling each situation with aplomb. If you can be there for your customer on the day he needs you most, you will truly have a customer for life.

Epilogue

As I hope to have illustrated with this recap of my 25-year journey, customer service is more than a 1-800 number or a department way in the back of the store. Customer service is an industry unto itself. Somewhere within every technology company, insurance firm, health care organization, government agency, and retail chain are a group of dedicated professionals chugging away solving customer problems, ever mindful of talk time, customer satisfaction, and first-contact resolution.

Whether you are a career service professional or just a customer interested in how service organizations work, I hope this book was useful and enlightening for you. In closing, I'd like to leave you with these final thoughts.

The Customer Is *Not* Always Right

I admit it, I'm a tough customer. I have high expectations for fast and easy interactions, and I am not as patient as I should be when things drag on too long, such as DIRECTV asking me to reboot my receiver (with a 15-minute reboot time) three times in a row, on a single phone call. And sometimes, I'm sorry to admit, I hear that tone sneak into my voice that borders on condescending, and I try to pull back and remember that this support agent is doing the best that he can, and me being snide is not going to help the situation.

The fact is, the customer is not always right, and oftentimes the support tech cannot do what the customer wants due to policy or procedure. In my experience, customer patience is running shorter and shorter; everyone seems on the brink of "losing it" on every interaction, and more customers today have a sense of entitlement that they may not deserve. When you encounter a service problem that is not being fixed to your satisfaction, consider following these steps:

- **Take a deep breath.** Ask yourself, "Am I being reasonable?" Think through the problem and your ideal resolution—are you expecting too much? Is what you want against the company's policy? As I illustrated in the Home Depot story, sometimes companies force customers to make a scene. But more often than not, making a scene is not going to help the situation, and you might just find yourself blacklisted from that company.

- **Write a letter.** I realize this habit is quickly fading into history, but I am a letter writer. I've learned that screaming at a Level 1 support agent is rarely helpful; the company will always protect their employees from abuse—as they should. If you are being treated unfairly, write a letter to the CEO's office and send it by registered mail. First of all, the act of writing that letter forces you to revisit the situation and all the facts, and I sometimes realize I am expecting too much and forget about it. But other times, sending that letter is far more cathartic than unloading frustration on a support agent. And guess what? A professionally written letter detailing the situation has, in my experience, about a 90 percent chance of the issue being resolved in your favor.

- **Be as vocal a fan as you are a critic.** If you are going to get on your pedestal and complain to the masses about slights in service, I trust you do the same thing when excellent service occurs. As I hope this book has illustrated, providing excellent service is incredibly complex, and companies that do a consistently good job should be lauded from the rafters.

Never Lie to Customers

I wrote a blog post once about a horrible experience I had with my local electric monopoly. After a series of storms, my power was out for several days. I called the utility company multiple times a day, holding for more than an hour each time, trying to get information. For 3 days I was told variations of, "They are working on it; it should be back on soon." Every time it was the same thing— wait a few hours and your power will be restored.

On the fourth day, my patience was running short. I had taken a long drive around my neighborhood and couldn't find any utility trucks working and began to wonder if I was being lied to.

I called the utility company again, held once more for over an hour to speak to a live person, and this agent finally told me the truth. "To be honest with you, sir, we haven't even sent anyone out to identify the problem. We are terribly backlogged due to the storm. It looks like a crew is scheduled to be out there tomorrow, so hopefully, they will identify the problem and get it fixed quickly."

Over 4 days I had spoken to at least a dozen different people, and every one of them had lied to me. With this one truth-teller on the phone, I asked him why I had been given wrong information by everyone else. "Some employees think it is easier just to tell customers what they want to hear," was his reply.

Never lie to customers. I don't care how bad the news is. Once you do, you have lost all credibility, all trust, and all good faith. I always suspected our electric monopoly was a coldhearted, profit-driven scourge on the public, and now it had been proved to me. As you can imagine, this impacts every dealing I have with the utility, and once again, I know I'm not as nice to their support techs as I should be.

Good Service Is Worth Paying For

I'm a big believer in maintenance plans. Yes, I know that just about every year *Consumer Reports* has an article claiming maintenance plans are a rip-off, but let me tell you, good service is worth paying for. Let's be realistic—consumer electronics firms do not make much money from you buying their products. The margins are incredibly thin due to competition, with big-box stores undercutting everyone and keeping prices barely above the cost to manufacture.

If you just bought a new smartphone, you probably paid $300 or more. How much of that ends up as profit for the manufacturing company? Maybe $20. How much does a customer support interaction cost? According to TSIA data, technical support issues resolved via phone have an average fully burdened cost of $246. If you call once for support, the company has lost money on the sale of the smartphone.

This is why you typically only receive unlimited service for the first 30 days after purchasing a product unless you buy an additional service contract. And I buy them every time and never regret it. I may be a tough customer with high expectations, but I don't expect stellar service for free. In fact, if I am struggling to get support from a company, one of the first things I ask is, "Is there a higher level of service available that I can pay for? Because this level of service is not meeting my needs."

A few years back, CRM and billing vendor Amdocs did a survey of consumers in the U.S. and the U.K., asking about customer preferences for service and attitudes about cost. Though mobile phone companies have one of the lowest loyalty rates in the world, with high customer churn usually linked to saving a few dollars monthly with a different plan, one of the findings of the survey was surprising. The majority of those surveyed said they were willing to pay an additional $5 to $10 a month to ensure better service, including little or no hold time waiting for an agent.

It turns out that the most cost-sensitive customers we know of—mobile phone users—are willing to pay more for better service.

Superior customer service comes at a price. My challenge to everyone who reads this book is to spend the extra dollars for the service contract and agree to join the "premier" level of service if one is offered, and if one isn't offered, write a letter asking that a premier service program be started. If you nickel-and-dime a company on support, don't complain when the service you receive doesn't fit your expectations. You get what you pay for.

And good service is worth paying for.

A Special Thanks Goes To...

First of all, I'd like to thank the individuals who encouraged me to write this book: Cindy McCombe, Lydia Zaffini, and Bill Rose. I mentioned a few names along the way of bosses, mentors, and co-workers who were especially influential in my customer service journey so far, but it was a very incomplete list. I'd like to thank everyone who has been so generous with their time and expertise over the years. In particular, some amazing folks at JCPenney who embodied "Love the Customer," Herm Brinkman, Judy Walden, and Dean Wortham. From my vendor days, a few Silicon Valley stars who gave me crash courses on everything from technology to marketing and product management, Sarah Nunke, Kirsten Berg Painter, Joe Davis, and Christine Crandell, who first encouraged me to become an analyst. From my analyst years, thanks to the visionaries who continue to inspire me, especially Erin Kinikin, Merv Adrian, Dan Mahoney, Elizabeth Herrell, and R. "Ray" Wang. I'd like to thank everyone who had a hand in making this book a reality, including Rosemarie Caserza, who helped shape my stories into a cohesive manuscript, and the team at TSIA who have been so helpful and supportive, J.B. Wood, Thomas Lah, Kira Sjoberg, Suzanne LaBounty, and Suzanne Hite. Last, but certainly not least, on the home front, thanks to Jay and Butters for your love, support, and most of all—your sense of humor.

Endnotes

Introduction

1. http://en.wikipedia.org/wiki/customer_service.

Section 1

1. http://money.cnn.com/2009/01/26/news/companies/home depot/index.htm.

Chapter 1

1. http://www.merriam-webster.com/dictionary/stewardship.

Section 2

1. November 11, 2011. "Oracle settles back pay claim." *San Jose Mercury News.* Section A, p. 4.

2. For more information, the official FLSA website can be found at http://www.dol.gov/compliance/laws/comp-flsa.htm. The document discussing the exemption for computer workers can be found at http://www.dol.gov/esa/regs/compliance/whd/fairpay/fs17e_computer.pdf.

Index

Note: Page numbers with *f* indicate figures.